Spend the Day in Ancient Greece

Spend the Day in Ancient Greece

Projects and Activities That Bring the Past to Life

Linda Honan

Illustrations by Ellen Kosmer

John Wiley & Sons, Inc.

New York • Chichester • Weinheim • Brisbane • Singapore • Toronto

This text is printed on acid-free paper.

Copyright © 1998 by Linda Honan

Published by John Wiley & Sons, Inc.

Illustrations © 1998 by Ellen Kosmer

All rights reserved. Published simultaneously in Canada.

Reproduction or translation of any part of this work beyond that permitted by Section 107 or 108 of the 1976 United States Copyright Act without the permission of the copyright owner is unlawful. Requests for permission or further information should be addressed to the Permissions Department, John Wiley & Sons, Inc.

The publisher and the author have made every reasonable effort to ensure that the experiments and activities in this book are safe when conducted as instructed but assume no responsibility for any damage caused or sustained while performing the experiments or activities in the book. Parents, guardians, and/or teachers should supervise young readers who undertake the experiments and activities in this book.

Library of Congress Cataloging-in-Publication Data

Honan, Linda.

Spend the day in ancient Greece: projects and activities that bring the past to life / Linda Honan; illustrations by Ellen Kosmer.

p. cm. — (Spend the day series)

Includes index.

ISBN 0-471-15454-7 (pbk. : alk. paper)

1. Athens (Greece)—Social life and customs—Juvenile literature. 2. Panathenaia—Greece—Athens—Juvenile literature. 3. Children—Greece—Athens—Juvenile literature. 4. Family life—Greece—Athens—Juvenile literature. I. Kosmer, Ellen Virginia. II. Title. III. Series

DF123.H66 1998

938'.5—dc21

Printed in the United States of America
10 9 8 7 6 5 4 3 2

In loving memory of my parents,
M. S. Honan, M.D., and Linda O'Connor Honan

In fond remembrance of my parents,
Michael Kosmer and Anne Minikauskas Kosmer

Acknowledgments

I would like to thank my colleagues and friends at Higgins Armory Museum, and the teachers and parents with whom we work, for their encouragement and forbearance. Particular thanks are due to our wonderful editor, Kara Raezer, for her patience and understanding. A long-overdue thanks to my father for the Greek primer he gave me as a summer project on our annual stay at the seaside in County Clare the year I was twelve.

—Linda Honan

I would like to thank my parents, who encouraged my youthful interest in the visual arts, and my colleagues at Worcester State College for their support and encouragement.

—Ellen Kosmer

Contents

INTRODUCTION

Welcome to Ancient Greece!

Imagine you could go back in time to spend the day in ancient Greece, the way it was then! This book will take you back over two thousand years to Athens, one of the most beautiful and important cities in the ancient world.

Athens is on the Greek mainland. To visit there long ago, you took a boat to the port of Athens at Piraeus (pronounced pie-REE-us). Then you walked about four miles (6.5 km) to the city itself. Along the way you passed large olive groves and fields planted with wheat and vegetables. You saw the red tile roofs of farmhouses peeking up here and there among the trees.

The road was crowded. Most people walked, but a few rich people rode horses. Farmers led oxcarts full of vegetables on their way to market. Merchants drove mule wagons piled high with goods for sale. Students came to study with the famous professors. Everyone who had the chance wanted to visit Athens, to see its magnificent buildings and art and hear a new play at the theater.

In this book you'll visit Athens during the high point of Greek civilization. It's summertime in the year 432 B.C., and the city is enjoying a holiday in honor of the birthday of **Athena** (uh-THEE-nuh),

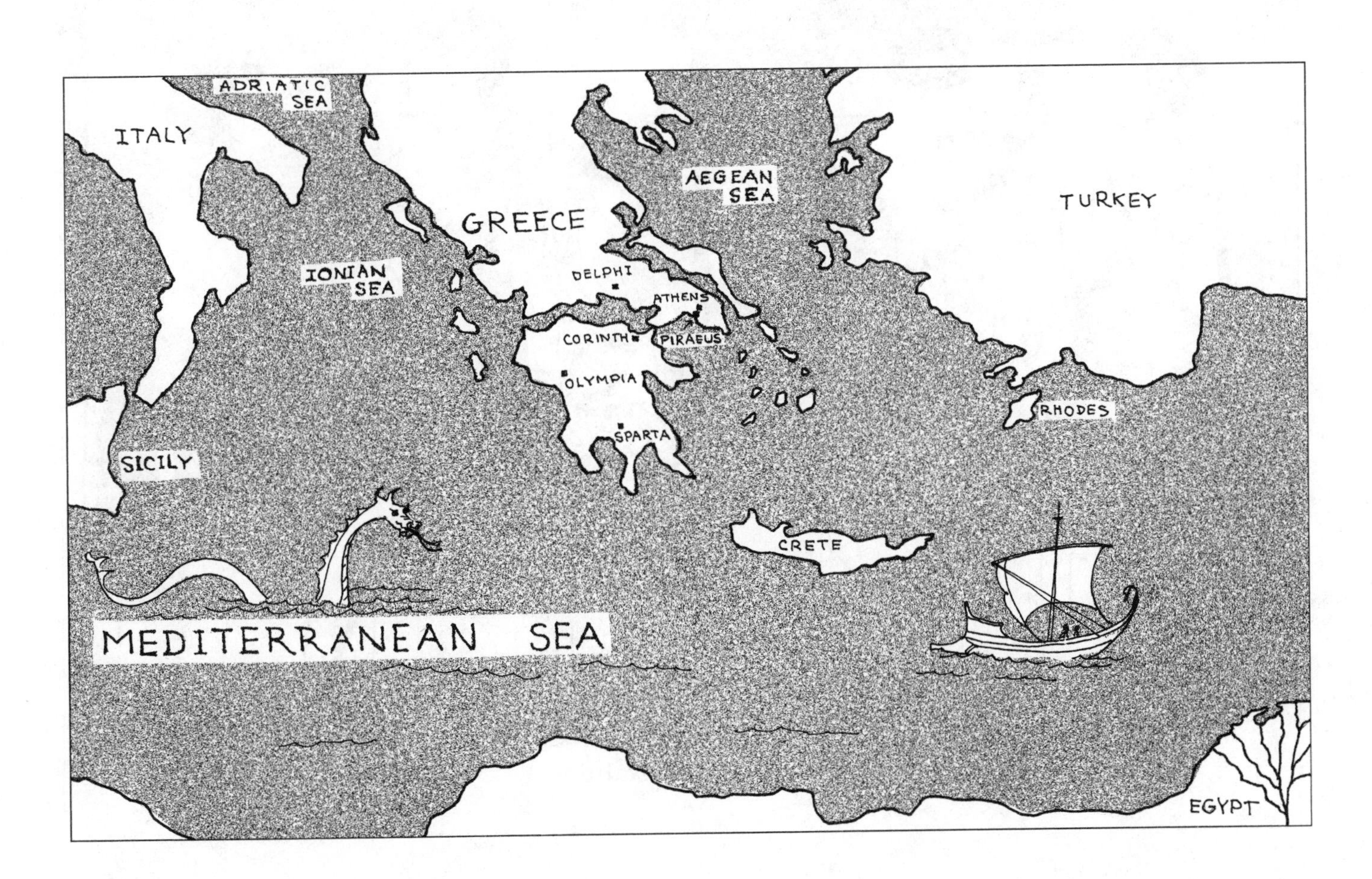

the goddess for whom the city is named. They celebrate with a festival called the **Panathenaic** (pan-uh-thuh-NAY-ick) **Games**, which means the games for all of Athens.

Thousands of years ago the ancient Greeks created a great civilization. The Greek world included the mainland and islands known today as Greece. It also spread west across what is now Italy and south as far as Egypt.

All the ancient Greeks shared a single language and religion, but Greece was not a united country. The Greek people lived in **city-states**, which were independent states ruled from one central city. Athens was a rich and powerful Greek city-state. It was also a center of education and learning. The people of Athens invented the idea of **democracy**, or political rule by the people.

The civilization of ancient Greece lasted from about 2000 to 200 B.C., and its high point was 500 to 300 B.C. During that time, the Greeks produced many important ideas about art, architecture, literature, politics, mathematics, and science. The last great ruler of Greece was Alexander the Great of Macedonia (356–323 B.C.). After him, Greece became politically weak, and was captured by the Romans in 146 B.C. The Romans spread Greek learning throughout their empire. Many of the ideas and beliefs of the ancient Greeks survived and are still admired today.

Meet the Family

In Athens you'll spend the day with a typical ancient Greek family: twelve-year-old Alexander, ten-year-old Helen, and their parents, Philip and Penelope. Alexander goes to school every day and

enjoys studying, but not as much as he loves sports. Helen's mother gives her lessons at home in housekeeping, reading, and music. Helen loves poetry and is a good weaver.

Alexander and Helen's father, Philip, is a doctor. He works in an office at the front of their house. Penelope, the children's mother, looks after the household. She cooks, weaves, and takes care of her children.

Two slaves live in the house: Cassandra and Myron. Cassandra was born a slave. She helps Penelope with all the housework. Myron was captured in battle ten years ago. He is in charge of Alexander's education.

Alexander and Helen's house is two floors high, with walls made from sun-dried bricks and a red tile roof. The windows are small, with no glass, and are covered with shutters. In the middle of the house there is an open courtyard, with a table called an **altar** where they worship the gods, pots with sweet-smelling herbs, and a well that gives plenty of cool water for Helen and Alexander to drink.

The Projects and Activities

In this book, you'll follow Alexander and Helen through their day, and along the way you'll do many of the things that they did. You'll make the kinds of clothes and jewelry they wore, write using their alphabet, prepare the kinds of food they ate, and much more. Through these projects and activities, ancient Greece will come alive. And you'll discover what life was like thousands of years ago for children just like you.

CHAPTER • 1

WAKING UP IN ATHENS

Helen wakes up early and jumps out of bed, not wanting to waste a minute of this wonderful day. Cassandra sleeps in Helen's room, too, on a blanket on the floor. She is already up, stoking the fire and fetching water for washing.

Helen pulls the blanket up neatly on her bed, and puts on a plain linen ankle-length tunic called a *chiton* (KYE-tuhn). She looks out her second-floor window at the *Acropolis* (uh-KRAH-puh-lus), a fortress on a hill in Athens, with strong stone walls enclosing temples. Later today she will go there for a ceremony and a feast, but first she must complete an important task. She must finish weaving a *peplos* (PEH-plus), a gown for a life-size

statue of the goddess Athena that she began nine months ago.

Helen worries that she will not make the peplos as beautiful as it should be. On her bedroom table a small statue of Athena stands guard. For luck, Helen touches the owl that the goddess carries.

ACTIVITY

ATHENA'S OWL

Athena was often shown with her owl in paintings and sculpture. The owl was a symbol of Athena's wisdom, and many owls nested on the Acropolis near Athena's temples. Make your own version of Athena's owl in this activity.

MATERIALS

several sheets of newspaper
1 pound (0.5 kg) self-hardening clay
resealable plastic bag
pen
strip of scrap cardboard
pencil

1. Spread the newspaper over your work surface.

2. Open the package of clay and squeeze the clay in your hands until it feels warm.

3. Divide the clay into three balls, one the size of a marble, the next the size of a Ping-Pong ball, and the biggest the size of a small orange. Put the two smaller balls into the plastic bag and seal it.

4. Make the owl's body.

a. Form the biggest ball into an egg shape.

b. Flatten one pointed end of the egg to be the bottom of the owl's body so the owl can stand. Place the owl's body on your work surface.

5. Make the owl's head.

a. Take the medium-size piece of clay out of the bag and reform it into a ball.

b. Place the ball on top of the body. Push down gently on the head to attach it securely to the body. Blend the clay down from the body into the head. Push down gently on the head.

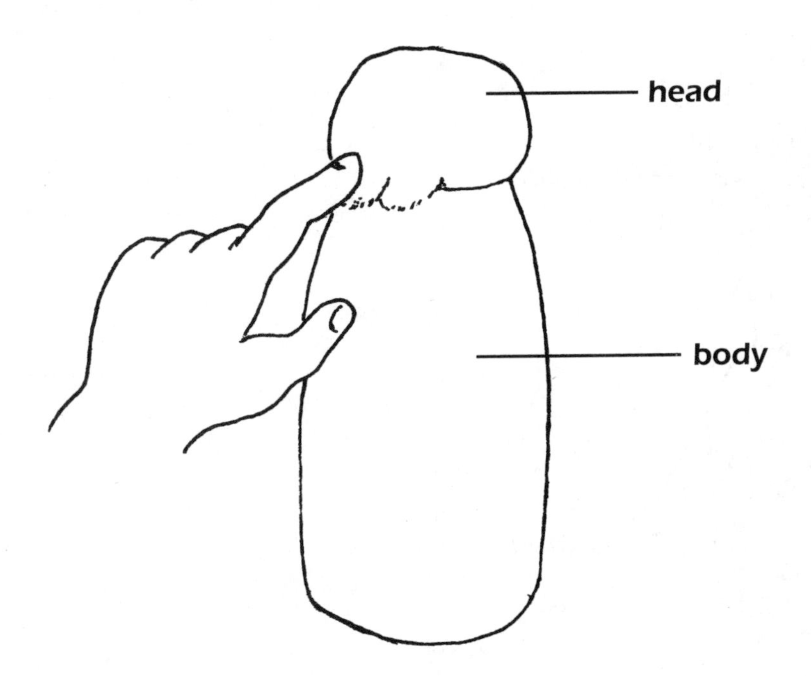

Gods and Goddesses

As a boy or girl in ancient Greece, you worshipped many gods by saying prayers and offering **sacrifices**, such as an animal or wine. You believed your gods looked like men and women but lived forever on top of Mount Olympus, the highest mountain in Greece. You learned about the gods from stories called **myths**.

You could tell one god from another by their symbols, which were special things that they wore or carried. Zeus was the chief and most powerful god, and his symbol was a thunderbolt. Athena was one of Zeus's daughters. She was the goddess of wisdom, of crafts, and of victory in war. Her symbols were the helmet and breastplate she wore and the owl and shield she carried.

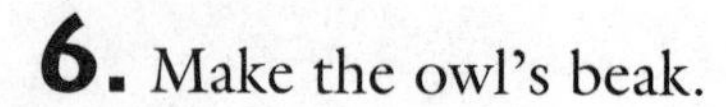

6. Make the owl's beak.

a. Take the smallest piece of clay out of the bag. Shape it into a diamond (◆).

b. Press the diamond-shaped clay onto the center front of the owl's head, smoothing out the clay where the pieces join together.

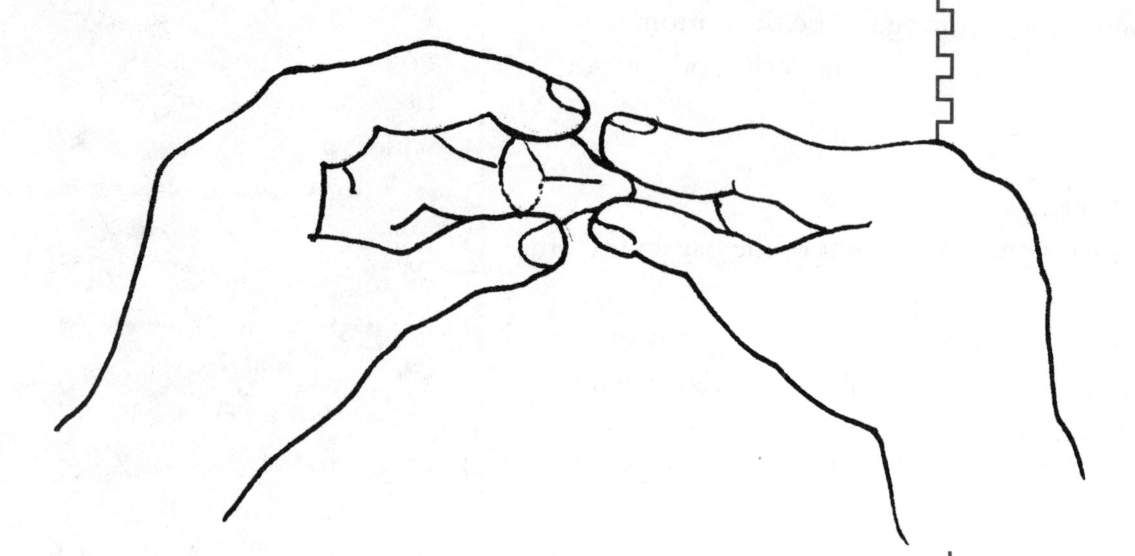

7. Decorate the owl.

a. With the pen cap still on, push the pen into the head at both sides of the beak to make the eyes.

b. Use the cardboard to draw circles around the eyes.

c. Use the pencil point to draw feathers on the front and back of the body and head.

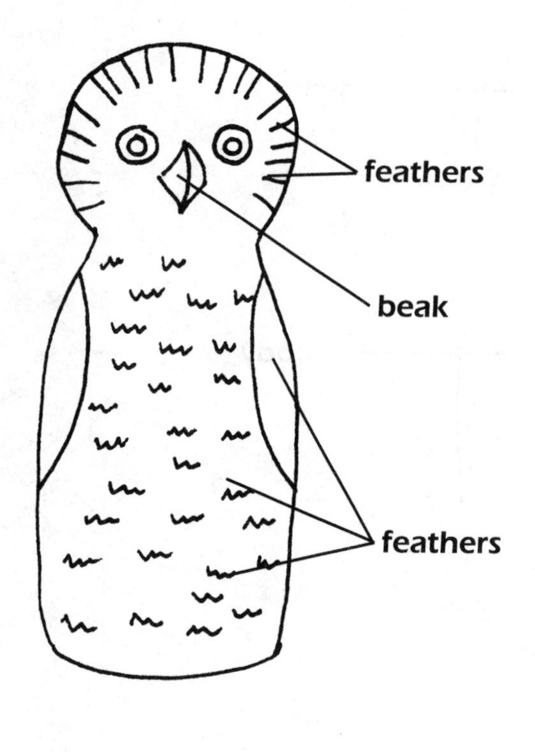

Like his younger sister, twelve-year-old Alexander has his own bedroom, which he shares with Myron. When Alexander wakes up, he lies in bed thinking about what he will do today. He is looking forward to the athletic contests. He hopes to buy a present for Helen's birthday, which is next week. And he can hardly wait for the great feast his family will share with the whole city tonight on top of the Acropolis.

Penelope calls to Alexander that it is time to get up. Alexander pulls on his linen chiton. He combs his hair and runs down the wooden stairs to the kitchen.

Greek Clothes

As an ancient Greek, you wore simple clothes made from linen or wool cloth. If you were a man or a boy, you wore a straight tunic called a chiton. It ended at the knee, and was pinned at the shoulders and belted at the waist. As a woman or girl, you wore an ankle-length chiton. Over it you often wore a long gown called a peplos.

Both men and women wore a woolen cloak called a **himation** (him-MAT-tee-un). Ancient Greeks usually went barefoot or wore sandals. For exercising and playing sports, men wore no clothes, and women wore a short chiton or nothing at all.

Activity

Chiton

The chiton worn by men and boys ended at the knee. In this activity, you'll make a short chiton, like Alexander's.

Greek boys and men often wore the chiton so that it covered only one shoulder, leaving the other bare. To make a one-shouldered chiton, undo the four pins at one shoulder, letting the extra cloth drape inside the tunic.

MATERIALS

scissors
white sheet or tablecloth
yardstick (meterstick)
8 diaper pins or large safety pins
needle and thread (optional)
3-foot (1-m) piece of rope
adult helper (if using needle and thread)

1. Cut the sheet to about 6 x 4 feet (2 x 1.3 m).

2. Fold the sheet in half lengthwise. Hold the sheet so that the fold runs down the side, as in the picture.

3. Use the pins to fasten the two halves of the sheet together. Fasten four pins at each shoulder as shown, leaving an opening in the middle for your head.

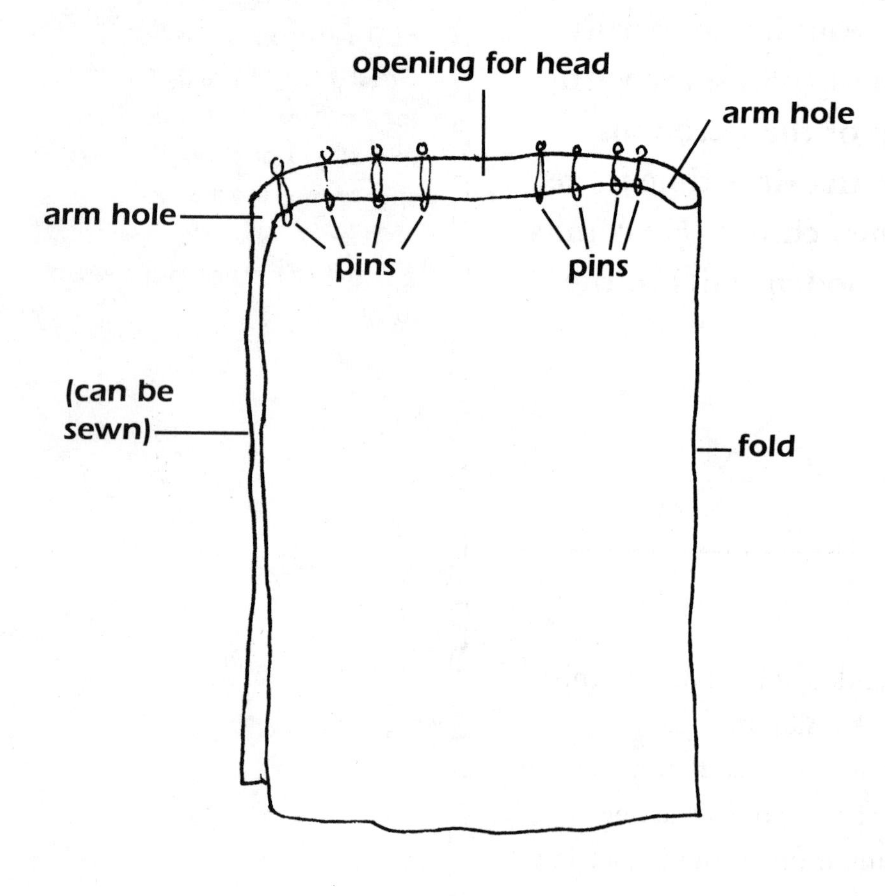

4. (Optional step) Have the adult help you use the needle and thread to sew the open side together.

5. Put on the chiton.

6. Tie the rope around your waist as a belt, then pull up the cloth above your waist, so that the chiton ends at your knees.

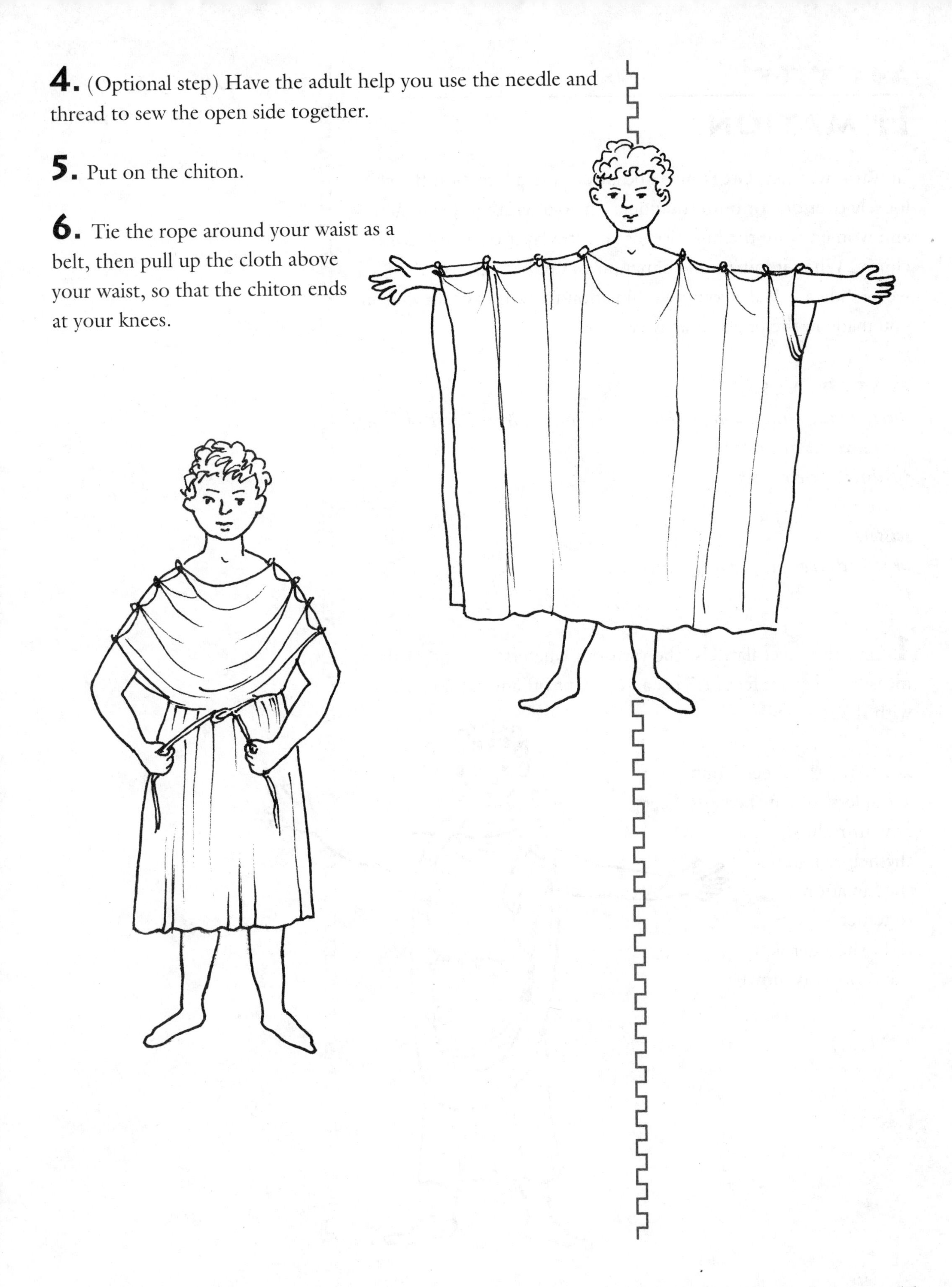

ACTIVITY

HIMATION

In warm weather, Greek men and boys wore a himation thrown loosely over one or both shoulders. In cold weather, both men and women wore the himation as an extra layer over a peplos or chiton. When it rained, the himation was pulled up over the wearer's head. Make your own himation to wear over the chiton you made in the previous activity.

MATERIALS

sheet, blanket, tablecloth, or fabric remnant at least 5 feet (1.7 m) square, in any color
yardstick (meterstick)
chalk
scissors
brooch, diaper pin, or large safety pin
helper

1. Lay the sheet flat. Use the yardstick (meterstick) and chalk to measure 5 square feet (1.7 m) across. Cut off any extra fabric with the scissors.

2. Wrap the sheet around your shoulders so that the ends meet at your right shoulder. Have the helper fasten the himation together at your right shoulder with the brooch as shown.

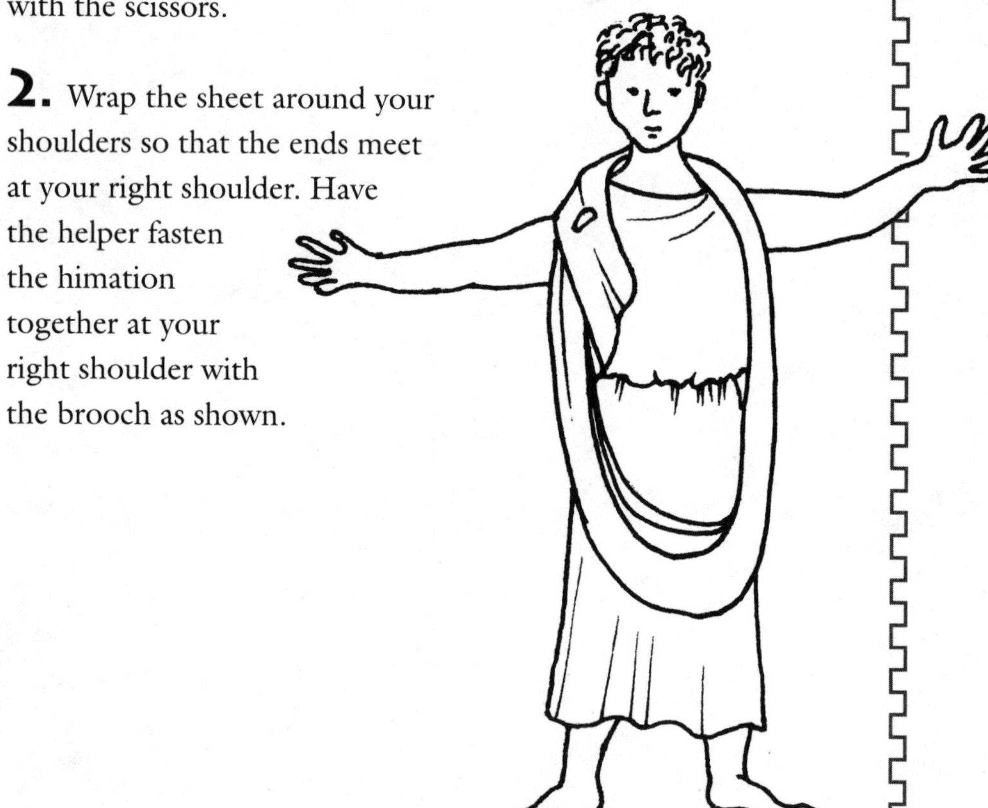

3. If you prefer, drape the himation over your right shoulder, then under your left arm. Have your helper fasten the himation together at the right shoulder with the brooch.

CHAPTER • 2

HELEN'S PEPLOS

As soon as she is dressed, Helen goes straight to the weaving room next to her bedroom. She must put the last touches on the special peplos that she is making. Helen's mother, Penelope, comes in to watch. Penelope sits in a curved wooden chair called a *klismos* (KLIZ-mus) and throws wheat to Helen's pet raven. Helen stands on a stool at the big wooden loom and weaves the gold-colored cloth. The smell of wool fills the room while she works. As she finishes each row of weaving, she tightens the cloth by pushing up a bar on the loom.

ACTIVITY

Loom and Weaving

The looms of ancient Greece were big wooden frames, taller than an adult, but you can make your own small loom to weave yarn into cloth.

MATERIALS

7-by-10-inch (17.5-by-25-cm) piece of corrugated cardboard, with the corrugation running the long way
ruler
pencil
scissors
scrap cardboard
4 yards (3.6 m) of white yarn
12 yards (11 m) of blue yarn

1. Make the loom.

a. Hold your cardboard with the short side on top. Draw a line across the cardboard ½ inch (1.25 cm) down from the top as shown.

Girls' Lives

As a girl in ancient Greece, your mother taught you to read and write, and to sing and play music. Your most important lesson was in keeping house, since you might be married at fourteen. Your social life was spent with your own family and your girlfriends. Your father and brother entertained friends in the dining room, but you never dined with men who were not related to you. Your friends visited you in the weaving room at the back of the house. You did not have the same rights as a boy. You could never be a citizen or vote in the governing assembly. Only freeborn men could be citizens and vote.

b. Starting ½ inch (1.25 cm) from the corner, draw a V ½ inch deep from the top edge of the cardboard to the line. Repeat every ½ inch (1.25 cm), until you have 19 V's. Cut out the V-shaped notches.
c. Repeat steps 1a and 1b at the opposite end of the cardboard.

2. Make the shuttle.
a. From the scrap cardboard, cut out a 3-by-1½-inch (7-by-3.5-cm) piece, with the corrugation running the long way.
b. On the cardboard piece, draw a line ¾ inch (2 cm) from each short end. Starting and ending ¼ inch (0.6 cm) in from the corners, draw a V to the line. Cut out the V's.

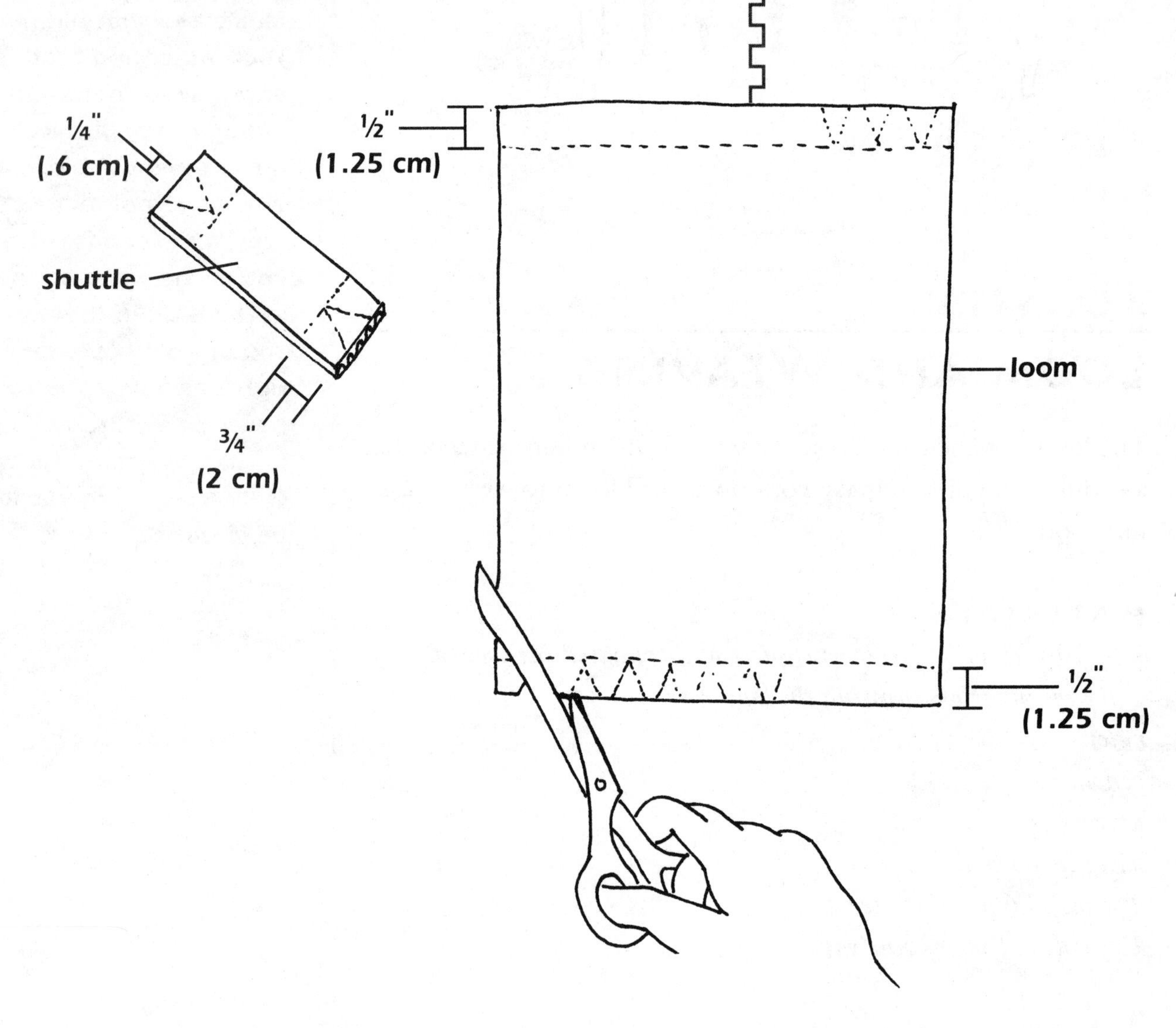

3. Make the warp (the yarn that runs up and down in the loom).

a. Tie one end of the white yarn around the top left projection of the loom.

b. Pull the yarn tightly down the front of the loom to the bottom left V-notch and loop it behind the second projection.

c. Pull the yarn back up the front of the loom to the top and loop it behind the third projection. Keep the warp stretched tight!

d. Continue up and down until all the notches are filled. Tie the yarn around the bottom right projection.

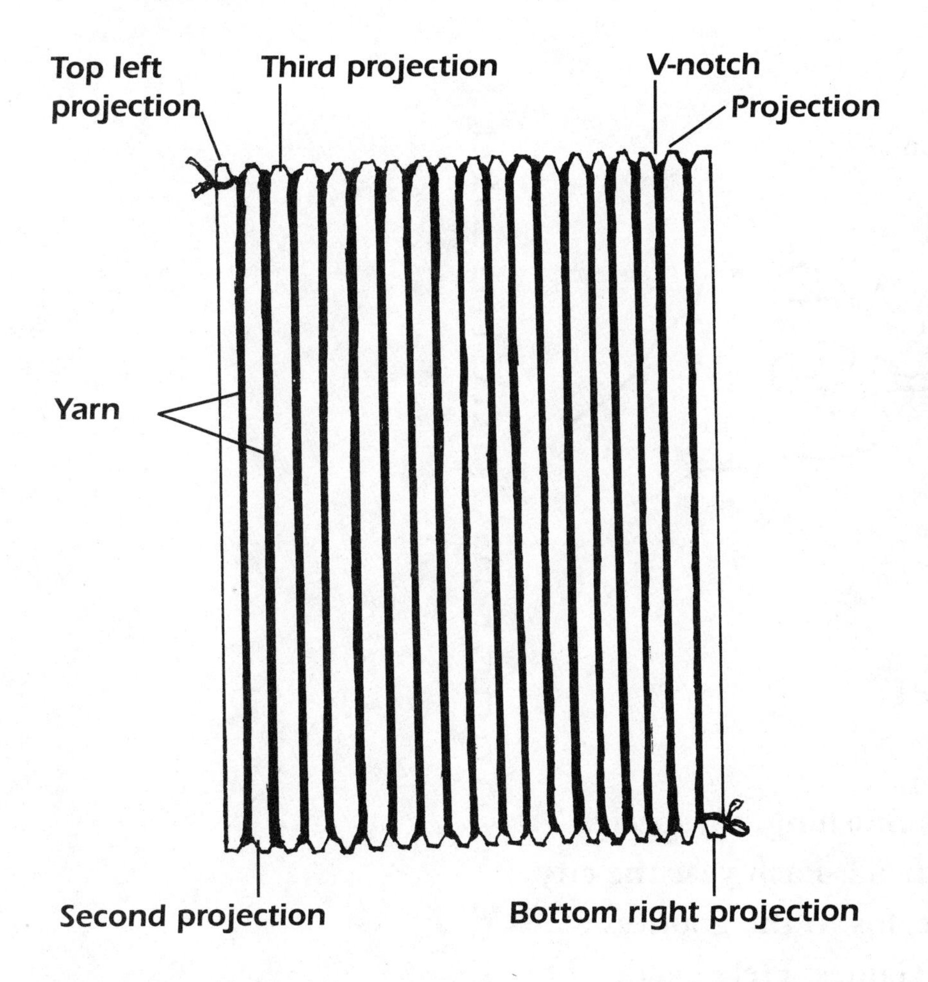

4. Make the weft (the yarn that runs side to side in the loom).

a. Take the shuttle and wrap the blue yarn through the shuttle's notches.

b. Starting at the center bottom row of the loom, weave your shuttle under and over each strand of warp as shown.

c. At the end of the row, weave over or under and come back to make the next row.

d. As you finish each row, push the rows together. Do not pull the weft too tight. Continue weaving until your loom is full.

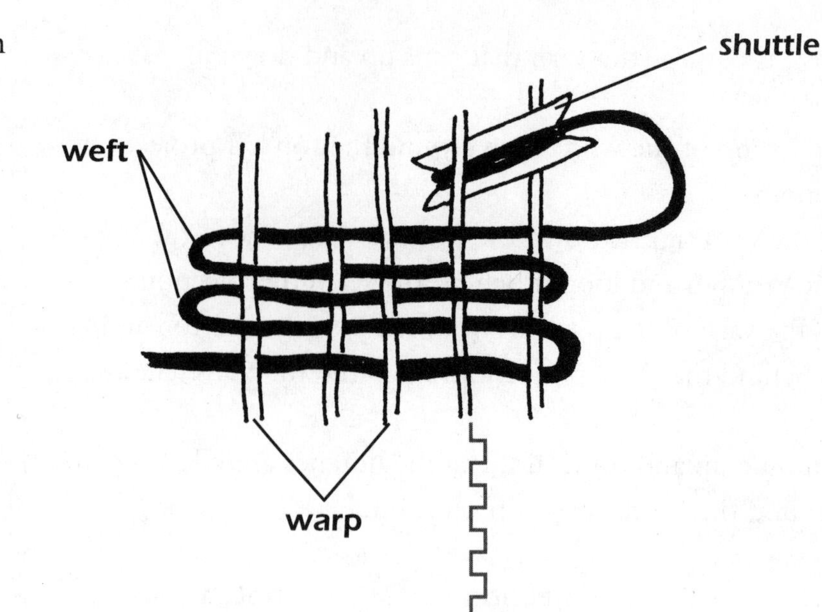

5. Take the weaving off the loom.

a. Carefully lift the first white warp loop off the projection at the top of the loom. Use the scissors to snip the loop, then tie the ends together as shown. Repeat across the top of the loom.

b. Repeat at the bottom of the loom.

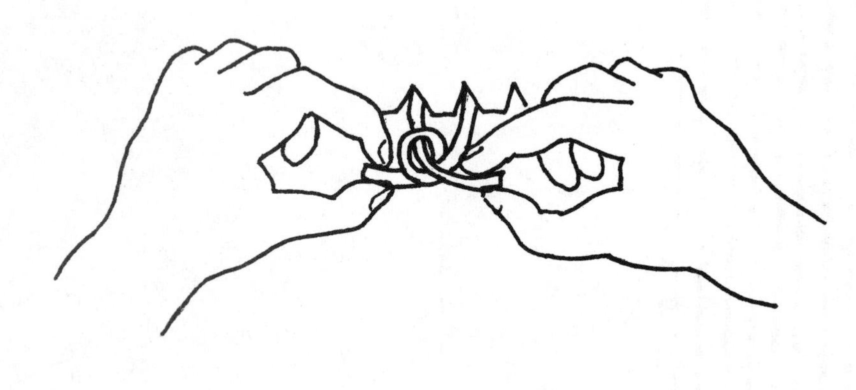

The peplos that Helen is finishing is a special gift for the goddess Athena. Each year the city of Athens presents a new peplos to the goddess at the end of the Panathenaic Games. Helen is one of four girls ages seven to ten who were chosen to weave the peplos this year.

Helen's peplos will be placed on a life-size statue of Athena that stands in a temple on top of the Acropolis. The peplos is made from gold-colored

wool, and down the center front are woven colorful pictures that show Athena and her father, Zeus, winning a great battle.

ACTIVITY

PEPLOS

The peplos was made of a rectangle of woolen cloth, pinned at the shoulders, with a capelike collar hanging down nearly to the waist. Use a sheet, tablecloth, or piece of fabric to make your own peplos.

MATERIALS

scissors
sheet, tablecloth, or piece of fabric at least 6 x 5 feet (2 x 1.7 m)
yardstick (meterstick)
2 diaper pins or large safety pins
2- to 3-foot (60- to 90-cm) rope

1. Cut your cloth to a piece 6 x 5 feet (2 x 1.7 m).

2. Fold down the top 18 inches (46 cm) of the cloth as shown.

THE PANATHENAIC GAMES

The Panathenaic Games were held every summer in honor of Athena's birthday. Every fourth year an extra-special celebration, called the Greater Panathenaia (pan-uh-thuh-NYE-uh), was held. The year 432 B.C. was one of those years of special celebration.

The games lasted a week and included both athletic events and contests in music, dance, and poetry. Only men and boys could compete in the Panathenaic Games. Women and girls watched the games, and had the important task of making the peplos for Athena. Women and girls had their own games at Olympia, in honor of the goddess Hera.

At the end of the Panathenaic Games, all of Athens participated in a parade and the presentation of the peplos to the goddess, followed by a great sacrifice and feast.

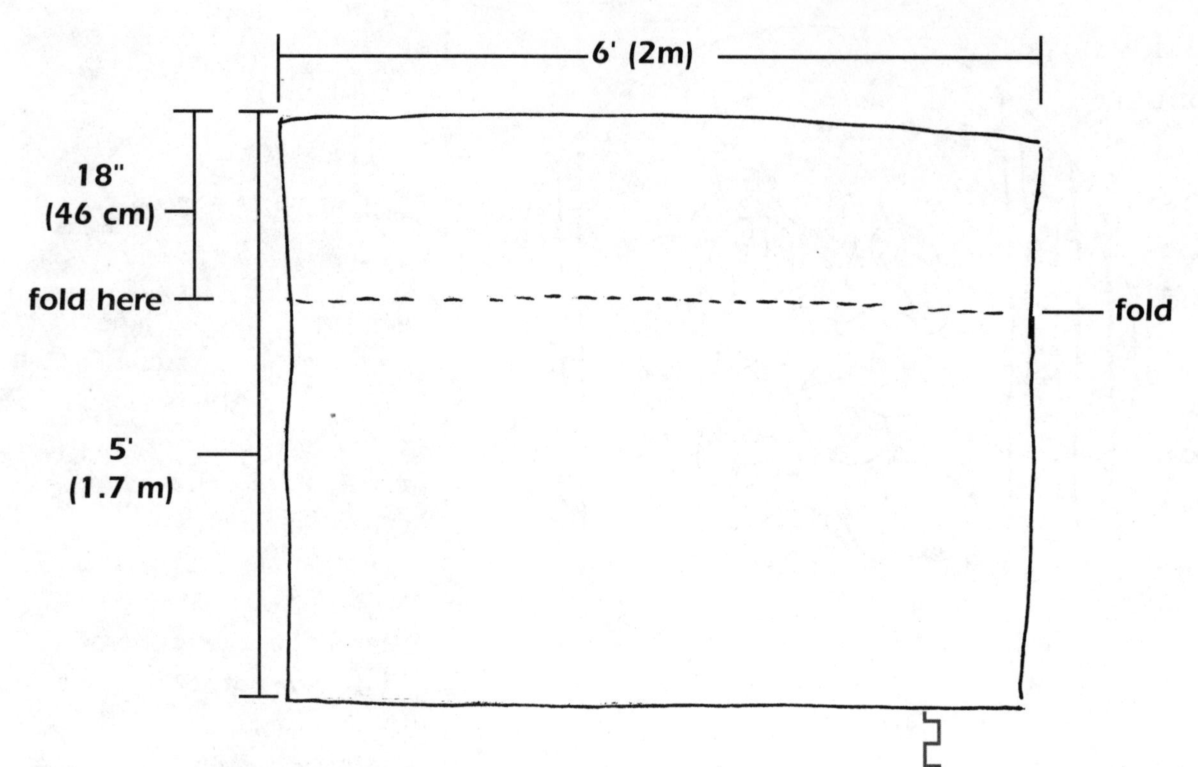

3. Fold the cloth in half lengthwise as shown.

4. Leave a hole for your head in the middle of the top fold, and fasten a pin at each shoulder.

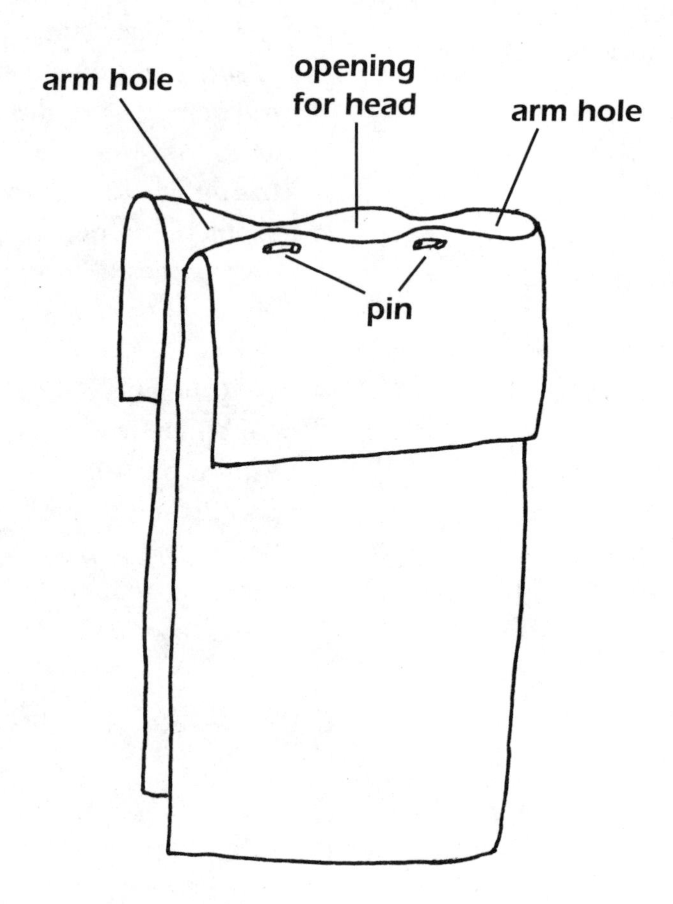

5. Put on the peplos and tie the rope around your waist for a belt.

6. Pull the cloth up above your waist, so the peplos ends at your ankles.

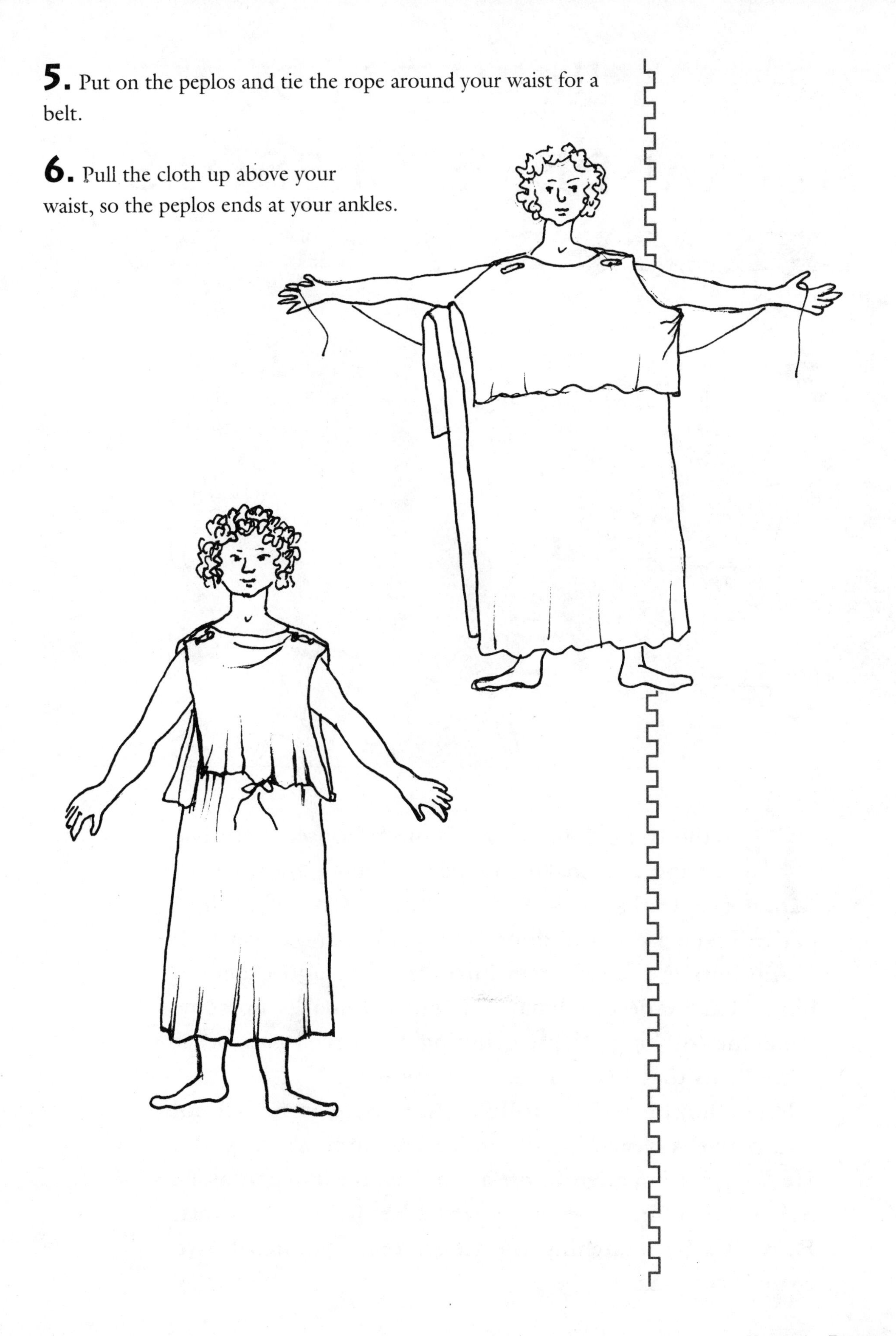

CHAPTER • 3

ALEXANDER'S LESSONS

By the front door of the family's house, there is a carving of a snake wrapped around a staff, to tell people that a doctor lives there. One of Philip's patients knocks at the door. The patient looks very ill. Philip hurries the sick man into his office and examines him. After he decides what is wrong, he makes up some medicine for his patient, grinding the herbs and other ingredients together to make a fine powder.

Even though it is a holiday and there is no school today, twelve-year-old Alexander has homework to do. He wriggles impatiently on a stool in the kitchen as he writes down lines of poetry that he has learned by heart. He writes by scratching the letters on a wooden board coated with wax.

ACTIVITY

WRITING IN GREEK

In this activity, you'll write in Greek, using the chart shown on page 24. In the chart, the letters in the two left-hand columns show the capital and lowercase letters of the Greek alphabet. The third column gives the letter name, and the fourth column shows the equivalent letter sound in the alphabet we use to write English.

MATERIALS

Greek alphabet chart
pencil
pad of paper

1. Read these rules for writing with Greek letters.
a. Use a Greek letter for each English letter or sound.
b. There's no letter in the Greek alphabet for the sound H, which occurs in Greek only at the start of a word beginning with a vowel. To show the H sound, as in "hot," place the mark ' over the vowel that begins the word, or in front of the vowel if the word is capitalized.

BOYS' LIVES

As a boy in ancient Athens, your most important duty was learning. You went to school from ages six to eighteen. You studied reading, writing, arithmetic, history, and music.

You took sports seriously and went each day to a sports field to run, wrestle, and throw the discus.

At age eighteen, you trained as a soldier in the Athenian army for two years. Then, if you could afford it, you studied with the philosophers, professors who taught every subject, including literature, science, mathematics, and medicine.

c. If a word begins with a vowel but has no H sound, as in "apple," place the mark ' over the first letter, or in front of the first letter if the word is capitalized.

d. Some other English letters are missing from the Greek alphabet. Use these Greek letters instead.

- For j, use ι .
- For c, use κ or σ (sigma is sometimes written s).
- For q, use κ .
- For v, use Φ.
- For w, use ου.
- For y, use ι or ευ.

THE GREEK ALPHABET

Capital letters	Lowercase letters	Letter name	English letter sound
Α	α	alpha	a (short)
Β	β	beta	b
Γ	γ	gamma	g
Δ	δ	delta	d
Ε	ε	epsilon	e
Ζ	ζ	zeta	z
Η	η	eta	a (long)
Θ	θ	theta	th
Ι	α	iota	i
Κ	κ	kappa	k
Λ	λ	lambda	l
Μ	μ	mu	m
Ν	ν	nu	n
Ξ	ξ	xi	x
Ο	ο	omicron	o (short)
Π	π	pi	p
Ρ	ρ	rho	r
Σ	σ (written s at the end of a word)	sigma	s
Τ	τ	tau	t
Υ	υ	upsilon	u
Φ	φ	phi	f
Χ	χ	chi	kh
Ψ	ψ	psi	ps
Ω	ω	omega	o (long)

2. Write your name using Greek letters. For example, if your name is Melissa, you would write Μελισσα (which means *honey* in Greek).

3. Write the name of your hometown using Greek letters. For example, if you come from Boston, you would write Βοστον. If you come from London, you would write Λονδον.

4. Use Greek letters to send a secret message to a friend and sign it with your name in Greek. For example:
Let's play ball after school.—Eric
Λετς πλαι βαλλ αφτερ σχοολ.—'Ερικ

ACTIVITY

GREEK NAMES

We still use Greek letter names for the names of college fraternities and in some sayings. For example, "from alpha to omega" means from beginning to end. "It's not worth an iota" means it isn't worth much. See if you can figure out the Greek words in the following activity.

MATERIALS

Greek alphabet chart from the previous activity
pencil
pad of paper

1. Use the Greek Alphabet chart to write out the Greek names below and guess what they are in English. Remember, some of them sound a little different in Greek.

a. 'Ελεν
b. 'Αλεξανδερ
c. 'Αθενα
d. Τροι
e. Φιλιπ
f. Πηνελοπεια
g. 'Ελλασ

SOCRATES AND PLATO

Two of the most famous Greek philosophers were Socrates and Plato. Socrates taught by asking questions, not by giving information. His questions were so clever that by answering them, people came to understand new ideas.

Socrates never wrote anything down, but his student Plato copied out many of his conversations. Plato taught students at a sports field near Athens called the Academy, which is why so many schools today are called academies. One of Plato's students was Aristotle, another important Greek philosopher.

h. Πλατων
i. 'Απολλων
j. 'Αθηναι
k. 'Αφροδιτη
l. 'Ηρα
m. Σωκρατης

2. Check your answers below.

a. Helen
b. Alexander
c. Athena
d. Troy (city the Greeks tried to win)
e. Philip
f. Penelope
g. Hellas (the Greek name for Greece)
h. Plato
i. Apollo (god of the sun, music, and health)
j. Athens
k. Aphrodite (goddess of love and beauty)
l. Hera (queen of the gods)
m. Socrates

ACTIVITY

CADUCEUS

In ancient Greece, doctors like Philip were known by a symbol: a carved staff with a single snake wrapped around it. In the Renaissance (around A.D. 1500), doctors adopted the **caduceus** (kuh-DOO-see-us), a winged staff with two snakes wrapped around it. Nowadays the caduceus is used to identify doctors, nurses, and medical technicians. You may see one displayed in a car, to show that the driver is a medical worker.

MATERIALS

2 pencils—one plain, the other unsharpened and with the outside colored red, blue, or black
4½-by-1½ inch (11-by-3.5-cm) piece of cardboard
scissors

ruler
6-by-6½-inch (15-by-16-cm) piece of gold or aluminum foil
transparent tape
two 12-inch (30-cm) gold tinsel stems or yellow pipe cleaners

1. Use the plain pencil to copy the wings in the picture below onto the cardboard. Cut out the wings.

2. Cut a 6-by-2½-inch (15-by-6-cm) strip from the foil.

3. Place the wings on the foil strip. Make cuts in the foil as shown by the dotted lines in the drawing.

4. Fold the cut foil over the wings, wrapping them tightly.

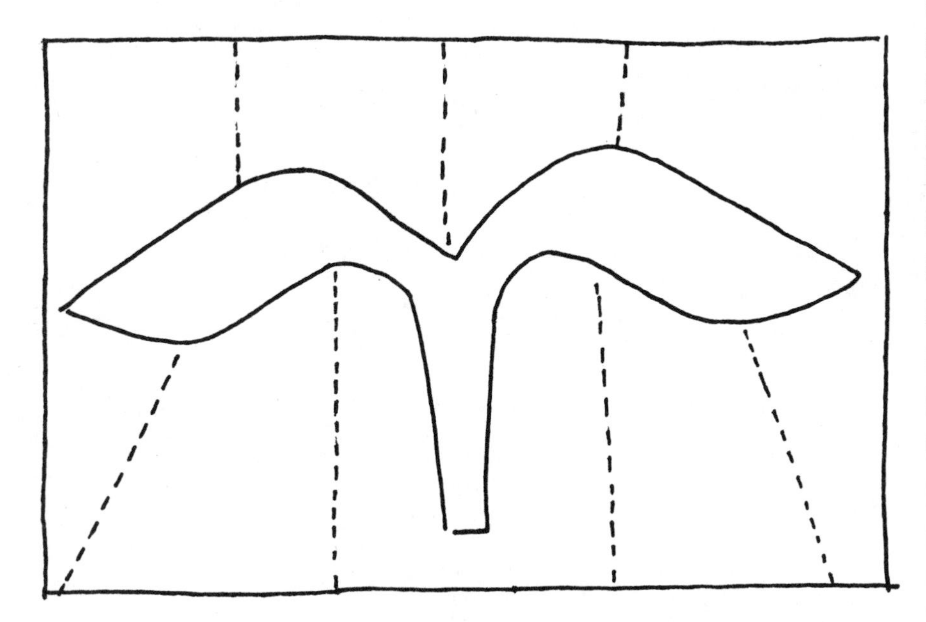

5. Place the top end of the colored pencil on the short end of the remaining piece of foil with about 2½ inches (6 cm) of foil sticking out above the pencil top.

6. Wrap the foil tightly around the pencil. Push the extra foil into a ball on the top of the pencil.

7. Place the pencil top in the middle of the wings. Use transparent tape to fasten the wings to the pencil so that the foil ball sticks up above the wings.

Hippocrates and the Hippocratic Oath

Hippocrates (hip-PAH-kruh-teez) was an ancient Greek doctor. He is called "the father of medicine" because he diagnosed many diseases and understood the connection between health, diet, and the environment. Doctors today still take his Hippocratic oath, a promise to use their medical knowledge only for their patients' good.

8. Wrap a tinsel stem around the pencil, starting 2 inches (5 cm) from the unsharpened end of the pencil. One-half inch (1 cm) away from the foil, bend the tinsel out and loop its end back to form a snake's head as shown.

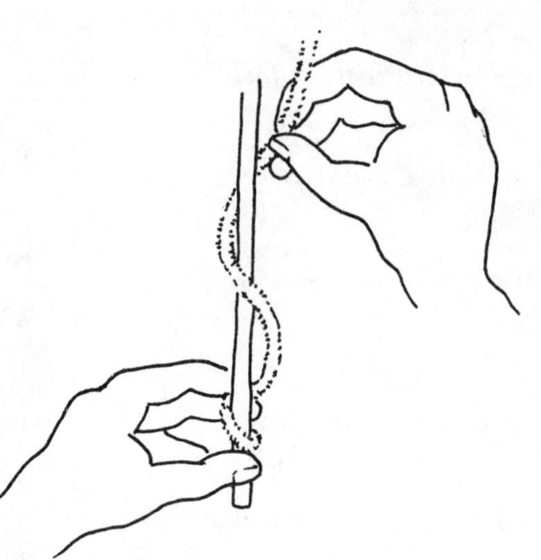

9. Repeat with the other tinsel stem, wrapping it in the opposite direction.

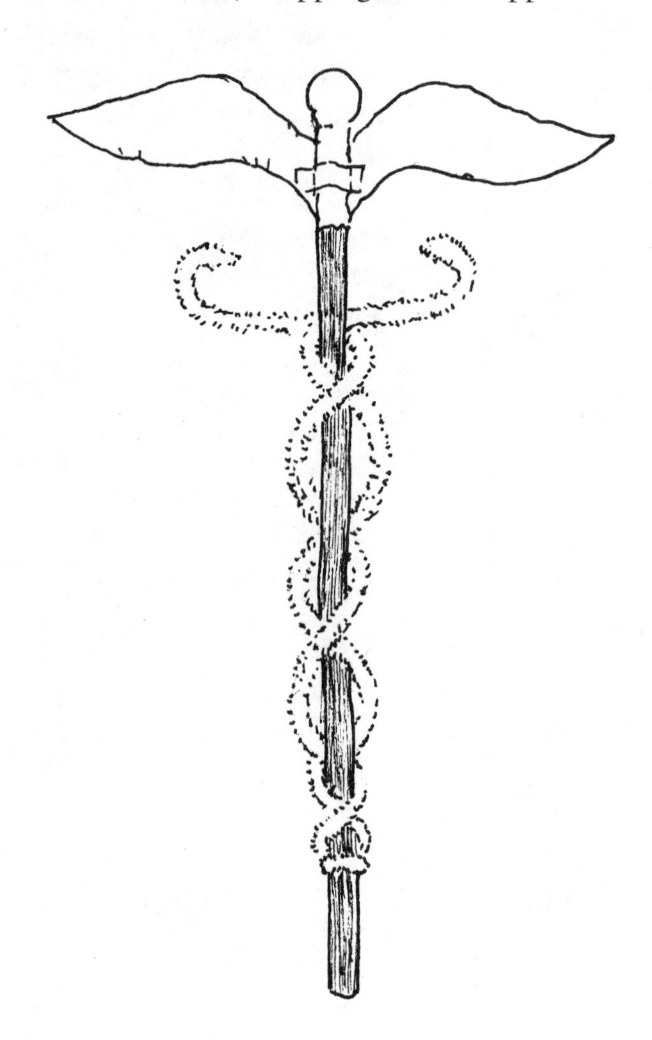

CHAPTER • 4

At the Theater

Finally, the office door opens and Philip's patient is shown out with his jar full of medicine. Now the family can go to the theater to hear the poetry contest. It is a short walk from their house to the theater, which is built into the southeast side of the Acropolis.

The outdoor theater looks huge to Alexander and Helen as they follow their parents down the stone steps to seats near the front. The front row is reserved for priests and officials, but luckily Philip finds seats only a few rows back. Even though it is still morning, about one quarter of the stone seats are already taken. When filled, the theater will hold fourteen thousand people.

As the family take their seats, the men who are competing in the poetry contest walk out to a large, flat space in front of the seats, called the orchestra. These men are professional actors, who travel from city to city acting in plays and reciting poems. Each of the actors wears a himation and an actor's mask, and holds a walking stick.

ACTIVITY

Actor's Mask

Greek actors wore masks over their faces to show the characters they played. The masks had open mouths to make the actors' voices sound louder. Some actors wore two masks at the same time, one over the face and one on the back of the head. By quickly switching masks, they could play two different characters in the same play, or show two different moods of the same character.

MATERIALS

9-inch (23-cm) white paper plate
pencil
ruler
scissors
fine-point marker, in black or other dark color

markers in black, brown, and red
one-hole paper punch
6 feet (2 m) of black or brown yarn or ribbon (optional)
2-foot (60-cm) piece of string or yarn

1. On the front of the plate, use the pencil to draw two small, round eyes, approximately ½ inch (1.25 cm) across. (Small eyes make you look more mysterious.)

2. Draw a large mouth, approximately 2 inches (5 cm) across and ¾ inch (2 cm) high. Curve the mouth down for a sad face, up for a happy face.

3. Draw a nose about 2 inches (5 cm) long.

4. Use the scissors to cut out the eyes and the mouth.

5. With the fine-point marker, draw around the eyes, mouth, and nose.

6. Use the black, brown, and red markers to decorate the mask. Draw in the hair around the top and sides of the mask. Draw eyebrows, ears, and any other features you choose.

7. (Optional) Make a beard.
a. Starting directly below the mouth, punch a hole ¼ inch (0.6 cm) in from the edge of the mask.
b. Punch a second hole ¼ inch (0.6 cm) to the right of the first hole.
c. Punch seven more holes ¼ inch (0.6 cm) apart along the lower right edge of the mask.
d. Punch eight holes ¼ inch (0.6 cm) apart along the lower left edge of the mask.
e. Cut the yarn into 17 pieces, each 4 inches (10 cm) long.
f. Tie a piece through each hole, knotting the yarn in front of the mask as shown.

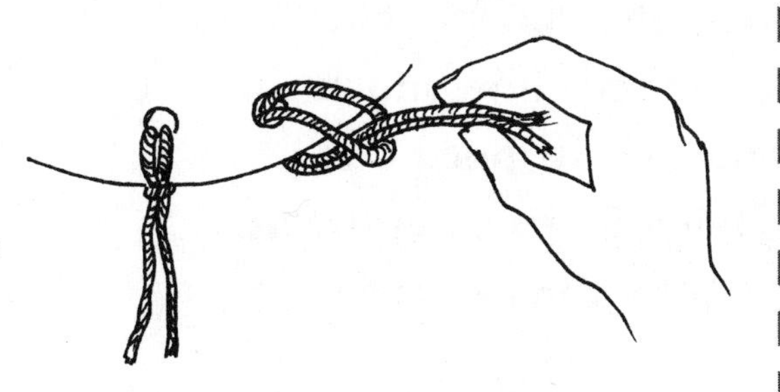

Music and Theater

As a boy or girl in ancient Greece, you were taught to sing and to play the flute and two stringed instruments, the lyre and the kithara (KITH-uh-ruh). Boys competed in singing and performing at the Panathenaic Games.

You often went to the theater with your parents. You believed that plays were pleasing to the god Dionysus (dye-uh-NYE-sus), and that hearing plays made you a better person.

You enjoyed two kinds of plays: funny plays called comedies that were about ordinary people and had happy endings, and serious plays called tragedies that were about gods and heroes.

8. Punch two holes 1 inch (2.5 cm) in from the edge of the mask near the tops of the ears.

9. Cut the 2-foot (60-cm) piece of string in half, and tie one piece to each hole.

10. Tie the ends of the string together at the back of your head.

A very dignified man wearing a handsome himation and holding a long, forked stick walks on to the orchestra. Penelope whispers to Helen that this man must be the judge, since a judge always carries a forked stick. The judge calls for the poetry contest to start, and the first actor steps forward.

The judge starts a water clock, and the actor begins to recite. Each actor in the contest is given the same amount of time to recite a poem. The water dripping out of the clock tells how much time he has left. When all the water has dripped out, his time is up. Alexander and Helen listen carefully as the actors recite verses written by the famous poet Homer.

Alexander and Helen and their parents enjoy listening to the actors recite Homer's poems about the Trojan War and its heroes. The best actor goes last. His voice booms out from his mask as he recites the story of the Trojan horse. Helen and Alexander clap and cheer when the actor finishes, and are glad when he receives the prize.

ACTIVITY

Clepsydra

The Greeks did not have mechanical clocks to keep track of the passing hours. But they did have a water clock called a **clepsydra** (KLEP-sye-druh) to measure short amounts of time. When someone performed in a contest or gave a speech in a law case or on politics, he was timed by the clepsydra. He had to stop as soon as all the water in the clock ran out.

In this activity you'll make your own version of the clepsydra. Use your water clock to time your friends in your own contest.

MATERIALS

masking tape
2 small, identical, wide-mouthed plastic bottles (such as empty and clean juice or water bottles)
felt-tip pen
thumbtack

scissors
clock or watch with second hand
pitcher of tap water
helper

1. Stick a small piece of masking tape on each bottle for labels. Use the pen to write A on one piece of tape and B on the other.

2. Push the thumbtack through the center of the bottom of bottle A to make a small hole. Remove the thumbtack.

3. With your pen, mark a line around the neck of bottle A.

4. Use the scissors to cut off a strip of masking tape long enough to run down the side of bottle B, and stick it on bottle B. You will mark the minutes on this strip.

5. Place bottle A on top of bottle B, holding bottle A in place for steps 6 and 7.

6. Tell your helper to watch the clock and signal you when the second hand is at 12. When the helper tells you, quickly pour the water into bottle A up to the line you made.

7. Have your helper continue to watch the clock and to tell you when each minute has passed. When 1 minute has passed, draw a line on the tape to mark the water level. When 2 minutes have passed, draw another line to mark the water level. Repeat every minute until bottle A is empty.

8. Write the number 1 on the tape beside the lowest mark on bottle B. Write 2 beside the next lowest mark. Continue until there is a number beside each mark.

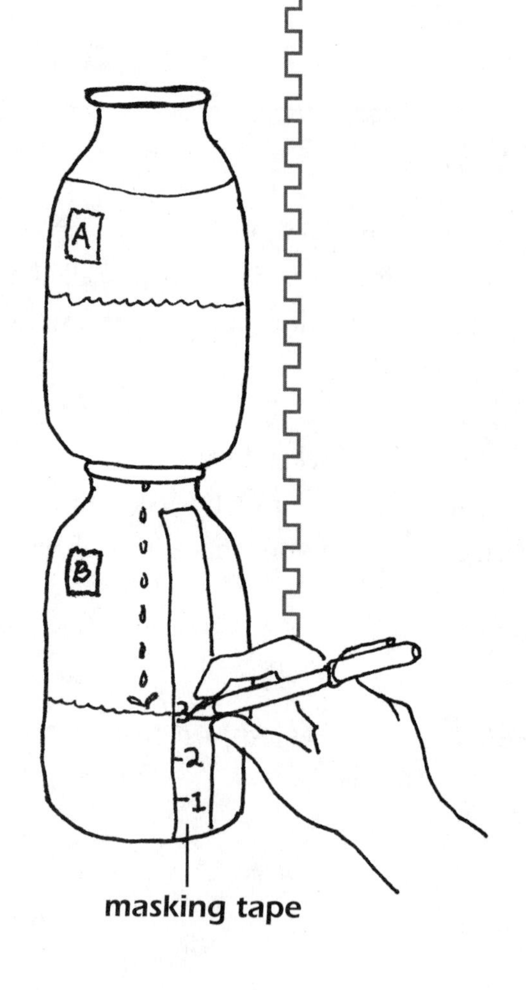

9. Empty out bottle B, refill bottle A, and place bottle A on top of bottle B as in step 5. Now you can use your water clock to tell how much time has passed!

ACTIVITY

TROJAN HORSE TREASURE BOX

The Trojan War was a conflict between Greece and the people of Troy long before Alexander and Helen's time. During the war, the Greeks built a huge wooden horse and placed it outside the Trojans' capital city of Troy. The Trojans thought the horse was a gift and took it inside their city walls. But the horse was filled with Greek soldiers, and during the night they jumped out and captured the city.

You can build a Trojan horse with a body that will hold all kinds of treasures. Make your horse natural-looking, or paint it in bright fantasy colors. What surprises will you hide in your horse?

MATERIALS

pencil
ruler
5 cardboard paper-towel tubes
scissors
duct tape
shoe box with lid
empty single-serving cereal box (from a multipack)
10-by-4-inch (25-by-10-cm) piece of cardboard
plastic drop cloth or old sheet
acrylic paint, regular or spray can, in any color
paintbrush (optional)

1. Make the first leg of the horse.
a. Draw a line completely around one paper-towel tube 2½ inches (6 cm) from one end.
b. Along opposite sides of that end of the tube, draw a line from the edge of the tube to the line going around the tube.
c. Cut out the section of tube along your lines as shown.

2. Make the other legs by repeating step 1 with three other paper-towel tubes. Save your scraps.

cut out

2½"
(6 cm)

3. Cut 34 pieces of duct tape, each 2 inches (5 cm) long. Rest these pieces on the edge of a table or other surface.

4. Make the horse's body.
a. Fit each corner of the shoe box into a cutout section of each leg as shown.
b. Fasten each leg to the box, using two pieces of tape for each leg.

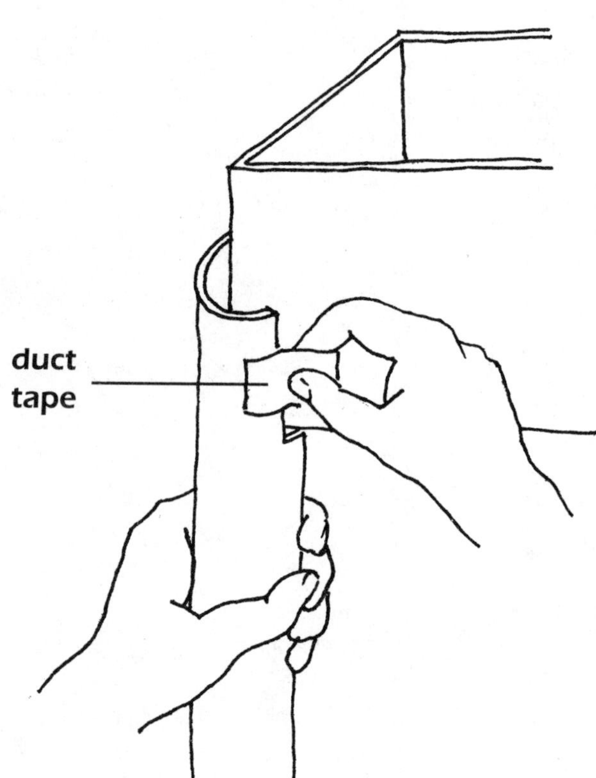

5. Make the neck.
a. Cut the last paper-towel tube down to 8 inches (20 cm).
b. Use the corner of a ruler to mark two 1-inch (2.5-cm) lines at a right angle on opposite sides of the tube end as shown. Cut out these two notches.

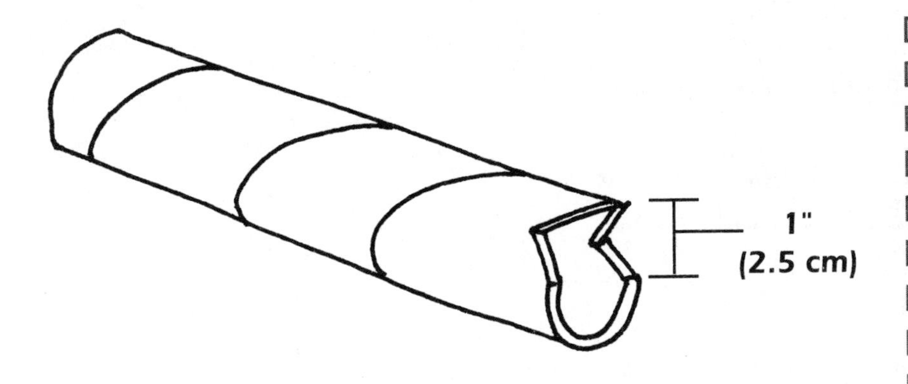

c. Take the lid off the shoe box. Position the notched end of the tube on one of the short sides of the lid.
d. Use four pieces of tape to fasten the neck to the lid.

6. Make the head.
a. Open the cereal box. Place the open end of the cereal box at the top end of the neck so that the box is 1 inch (2.5 cm) higher than the neck.
b. Wrap the box flaps around the neck, and use eight pieces of duct tape to fasten the head to the neck.

7. Make the ears.
a. Using the cardboard scraps from step 2, cut two triangles 2 x 1½ inches (5 x 3.5 cm).
b. Cut a ½-inch (1.25-cm) slit at the center base of each triangle.
c. Slide the ears over the cereal box flaps as shown on page 38. Tape each ear to a flap with a piece of duct tape.

8. Make the mane.
a. Cut the rectangular piece of cardboard in half, to make two 10-by-2-inch (25-by-5-cm) pieces.
b. On one piece of cardboard, use the pencil to copy the mane in the picture and cut it out.
c. Use eight pieces of tape to fix the mane on the neck, with the narrow end of the mane at the top.

Homer and Sappho

The most famous Greek poet is Homer. Nothing certain is known about Homer, although historians believe that he lived about 700 B.C. and that he was blind. Homer wrote two long poems called The Iliad and The Odyssey, which tell stories about the Trojan War.

Sappho (sa-FO) was a great Greek female poet who lived about 600 B.C. While Homer was famous for writing long poems about wars and heroes, Sappho was admired for short verses about friendship and love, which people still enjoy reading today.

9. Make the tail.

a. Cut 2 inches (5 cm) off the remaining piece of cardboard, to make it 8 x 2 inches (20 x 5 cm).

b. Copy the tail in the picture on the cardboard, and cut it out.

c. Put the wide end of the tail at the top. Use the remaining four pieces of duct tape to fasten the tail to the body of the box, not to the lid.

10. Stand the horse on the plastic drop cloth and paint it, using spray paint or a paintbrush.

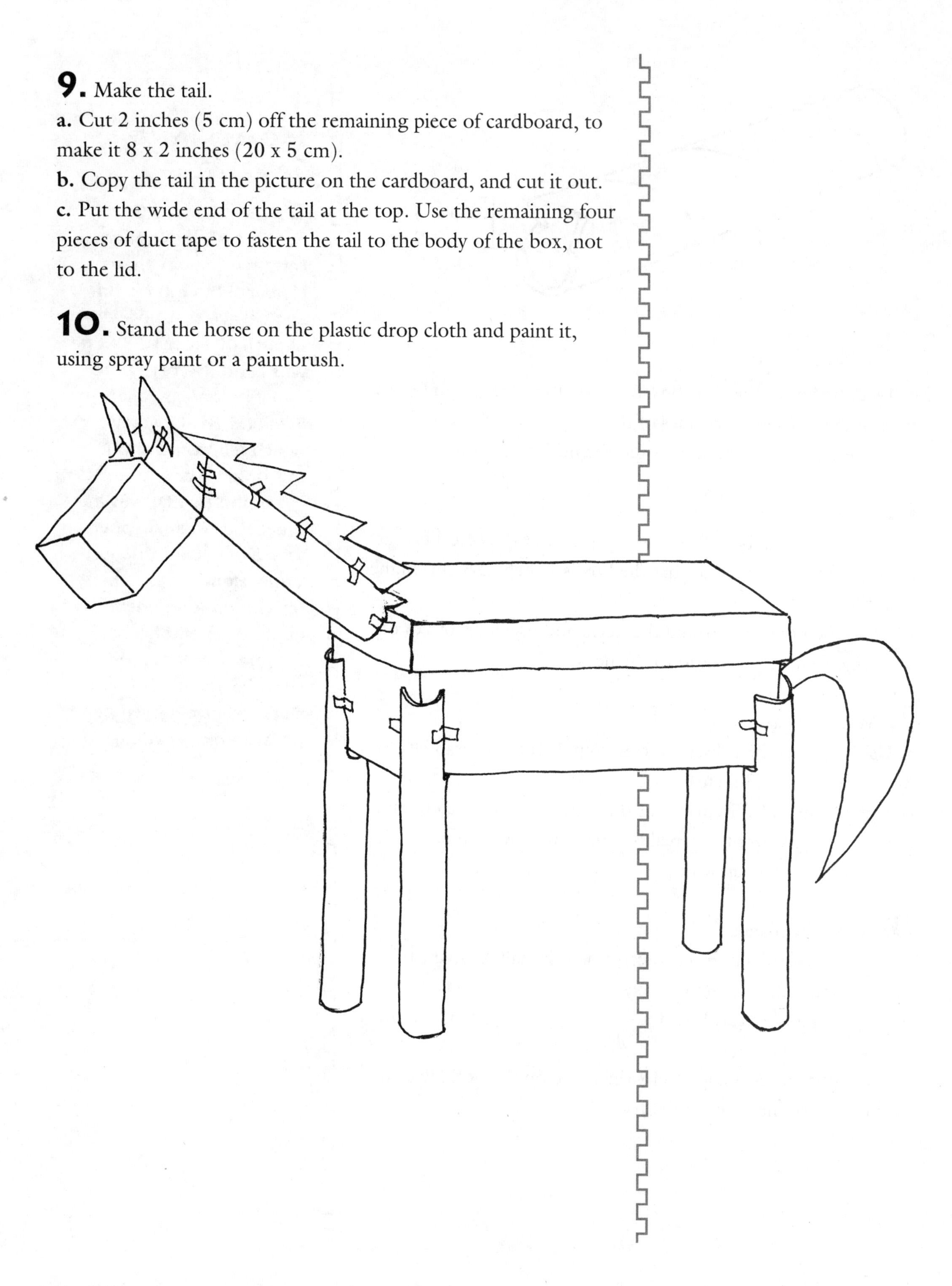

CHAPTER • 5

Lunch in the Agora

At noon, Penelope and Helen leave the theater and return home to get ready for the evening events. Philip and Alexander go to the marketplace, called the *agora* (AG-guh-ruh), to have lunch and watch the athletic contests. Along two sides of the agora there are long porches, called *stoas*, that have stone roofs and *columns*. The market sellers' stalls are in the stoas, sheltered from sun and rain. In the middle of the agora, a racetrack has been marked out. Wooden stands have been set up next to the track for viewing the races and other games.

Philip finds a place for him and Alexander to sit. He gives Alexander some coins from his purse to buy lunch.

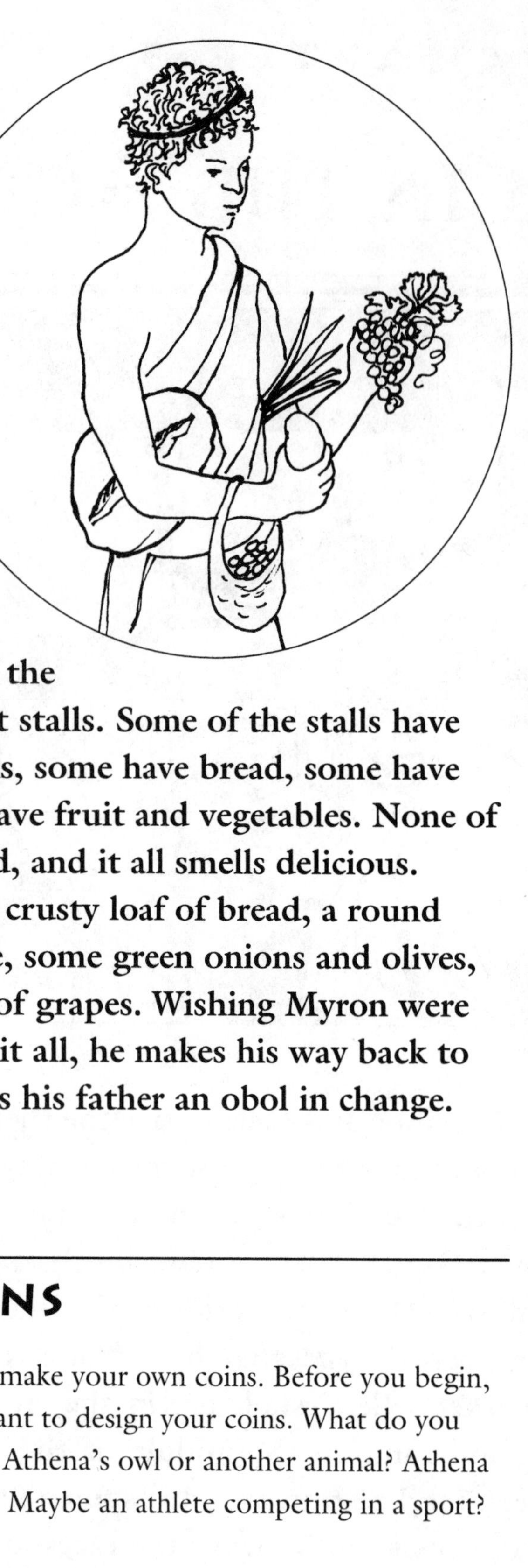

Alexander looks at the coins: he has three drachmas (DRACK-muz) and two obols (AH-bulz). He can buy a really good lunch!

Holding his coins tightly, Alexander skips around the edge of the agora to the market stalls. Some of the stalls have grilled fish on sticks, some have bread, some have cheese, and some have fruit and vegetables. None of the food is wrapped, and it all smells delicious.

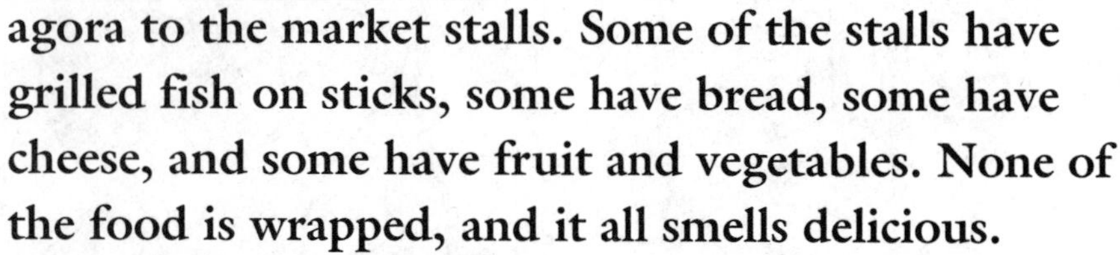

Alexander buys a crusty loaf of bread, a round white ball of cheese, some green onions and olives, and a small bunch of grapes. Wishing Myron were there to help carry it all, he makes his way back to the stands and gives his father an obol in change.

ACTIVITY

GREEK COINS

In this activity, you can make your own coins. Before you begin, think about how you want to design your coins. What do you want to show on them? Athena's owl or another animal? Athena herself or another hero? Maybe an athlete competing in a sport?

MATERIALS

bottle caps in several sizes
cardboard scraps

pencil
scissors
black marker

1. Put a bottle cap on the cardboard and draw around it in pencil.

2. Cut out the circle. This will be your coin.

3. Draw a design on each side of your coin in pencil. Write the name of your city on one side of the coin in Greek letters. (Use the Greek alphabet chart from the "Writing in Greek" activity in chapter 3.) If your city has a long name, just give the first three or four letters—coins made in Athens just said ΑΘΕ.

4. Go over your drawing and letters with the marker.

5. Repeat steps 1 through 4, using different-size bottle caps to make different-size coins. Try different designs. Make as many coins as you want!

"OWL" of ATHENS

Owl

Coins

If you went shopping in ancient Greece, you needed to bring a purse full of coins with you. You had no paper money, no checks, and no credit cards!

Each Greek city-state made its own silver coins. The city name was stamped on each coin, along with a picture of something connected with the city. Coins made in Athens were called **owls**, because they showed the head of Athena on one side, and her symbol, the owl, on the other side, with an olive branch. There were three values of coins: the **stater**, the **drachma**, and the **obol**. The stater equaled two drachmas, and the drachma equaled six obols.

A wine seller sees Philip and Alexander beginning to eat and comes over. Philip buys a small flask of wine and a big jug of water. They pour water into the wine, and eat and drink contentedly as they watch young boys compete in the *pentathlon* (pen-TATH-lun). Penta is the Greek word for five, and the pentathlon consists of five events: running, jumping, wrestling, throwing a long stick called the *javelin*, and throwing a round disk made of metal or stone called the discus.

To win the pentathlon, the winner has to score highest in three of the events. Alexander cheers when the boy who had won the wrestling also wins the javelin contest and finally the discus contest, too. He is the winner of the whole pentathlon! As he claps, Alexander decides to train hard so he can compete in next year's games.

Sitting next to Philip and Alexander in the stands is an old man wearing a dried-up leafy wreath on his head. Alexander looks at him respectfully. He knows the man is an athlete and that he won his wreath at one of the *Crown Games*, the biggest and most prestigious games in all of Greece.

ACTIVITY

Discus

In the pentathlon, boys threw a smaller and lighter discus than men. The boys' discus measured about eight and a half inches (21.5 cm) in diameter and weighed about one pound (0.5 kg).

Make your own version of a boy's discus. Decorate it with Greek designs and sign your name in Greek letters.

MATERIALS

several sheets of newspaper
pencil
9-inch (23-cm) paper plate
small paintbrush
poster paints in several colors of your choice

1. Spread newspaper over your work surface.

2. Copy the design shown here onto the back of the plate.

3. Paint the design in the colors of your choice.

4. Sign your work by painting your name in Greek letters.

5. Let the paint dry, then have a contest to see who can throw your discus farthest!

ACTIVITY

WINNER'S CROWN

Most games in ancient Greece were local, like the Panathenaic Games, which were for the people of Athens. But there were also national games called the **Panhellenic** (pan-huh-LEH-nick) **Games**, which means the games that were open to all Greeks. These were also called the Crown Games, because of the wreath or leafy crown awarded to winners.

At each of the Crown Games, the winners' wreaths were made of a particular plant: celery leaves at Corinth; laurel or bay leaves at Delphi (DELL-fie); parsley leaves or pine needles at Nemea (NEE-me-uh); and olive leaves at Olympia. Make your own wreath and wear it to show you are a winner, too!

MATERIALS

one-hole paper punch
1-by-22½-inch (2.5-by-56.25-cm) strip of cardboard
ruler
pencil
scissors
18-inch (45-cm) narrow ribbon
small branches, each about 3 to 4 inches (7.5 to 10 cm) long, of real or artificial plants

1. Using the paper punch, punch a hole at each end of the cardboard strip, ½ inch (1.25 cm) in from the ends.

2. Use the pencil and ruler to draw a series of lines centered along the length of the cardboard strip. Starting 1 inch (2.5 cm) from the end, draw 1-inch (2.5-cm) lines with ½-inch (1.25-cm) spaces between them, as shown.

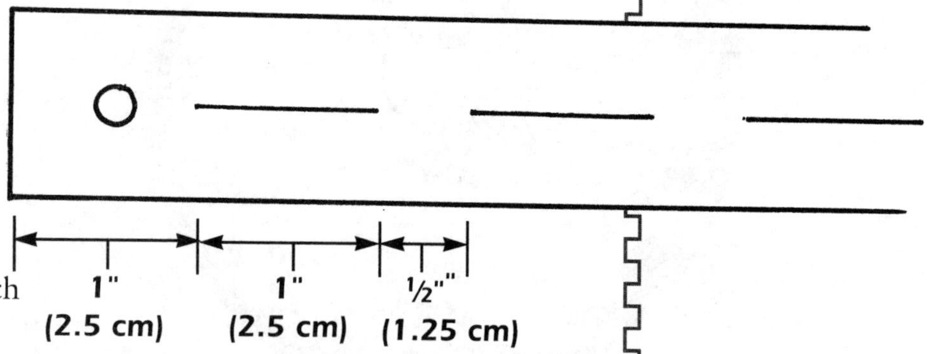

1" (2.5 cm)
1" (2.5 cm)
½" (1.25 cm)

3. Cut through each of the 1-inch (2.5-cm) lines. If you find it hard to start each cut, use the paper punch to make a starter hole at one end of the line.

4. Tie the ribbon loosely through the punched hole in each end and try your wreath on for size. If it is too large, move one end of the ribbon to one of the slits you cut in step 2, and cut off the extra cardboard. If it is too small, extend the ribbon and leave some space between the ends of the cardboard.

5. When the size is right, take off the wreath carefully and tie the ribbon in a bow.

6. Push the stems of your plant through each slit in the cardboard. Pull them through firmly so that the branches won't fall out when you put the crown back on your head.

7. Put your winner's crown back on your head and wear it proudly!

Olympic Games

The first **Olympic Games** were the Crown Games held at the **shrine**, or site for worship, of the great god Zeus at Olympia in 776 B.C. The Crown Games were for men and boys only. A separate series of games for girls and women was held at a different time at Olympia in honor of the goddess Hera. The modern Olympic Games were started in 1896 by a Frenchman, Baron Pierre de Coubertin. The modern games are open to men and women, and to athletes from all over the world. But unlike the ancient Greek games, the modern Olympic Games don't include special contests for children and teenagers.

CHAPTER • 6

The Chariot Race

While Alexander and Philip watch the pentathlon, other athletic events are going on all over the city. One of the most popular events is the *chariot* race.

The chariot race is taking place at the *hippodrome,* the racetrack a short distance outside the city walls. The hippodrome is a big field, eight times the length of the agora. Today it is filled with thousands of excited people, sitting and standing in the hot sun on a rise next to the track. The sharp smell of crushed grass fills the air as the people crowd in as close as they can.

Many well-known people of Athens are there, wearing elegant clothes and rich jewelry. Only wealthy people can afford to own racing chariots and horses. If they have enough money, even women can own race-horses. This is because the owners of the horses do not drive their own chariots; instead they hire drivers.

In some races the chariots are drawn by four horses, but today's race is for two-horse chariots. The light, wooden, two-wheeled chariots line up at one end of the field, where a row of judges in purple robes oversees the start of the race. The horses snort and paw the ground nervously as their drivers try to keep them in line.

Then a trumpet sounds, the crowd cheers, and they're off! The horses' hooves pound the earth as they start down the track. Wearing white tunics, the drivers stand in their chariots, guiding them skillfully so that they will not crash into one another or turn over as they round the bend at the end of the field. Each chariot is painted a different bright color—blue, red, white, green, gold, or purple—so the crowd can tell them apart even when they are far away.

ACTIVITY

RACING CHARIOT

Sometimes the movies show very fancy ancient racing chariots made of metal, usually bronze. But the Greeks actually raced in light, wooden chariots. The Greeks used oxen and mules to pull plows and farm wagons. They valued horses for speed and used them to pull light racing chariots. The chariot in this activity is a two-horse model.

Your chariot will be made from a cardboard cereal box, with a pencil for the axle, the thin bar around which the wheels spin. It also has a cardboard shaft, the bar to which the horses are harnessed.

MATERIALS

family-size cereal box
pencil
ruler
scissors
3-inch (7.5-cm) -diameter round can, such as a tuna fish can
3-by-6-inch (7.5-by-15-cm) piece of corrugated cardboard
black felt-tip marker
4½-by-1-inch (11.25-by-2.5-cm) piece of thin cardboard
short, unsharpened pencil, about 1 inch (2.5 cm) longer than the width of the cereal box
white glue or glue gun (The glue gun is to be used only by an adult.)
adult helper (if using glue gun)

1. Make the body of the chariot.

a. Lay the cereal box on your work surface with the front faceup. Along the bottom, mark a point 3 inches (7.5 cm) from the lower right corner. Mark another point 4 inches (10 cm) up from the corner along the side. Draw lines connecting these marks as shown.

b. Turn the cereal box over. Mark the same points on the lower left corner and again draw connecting lines.

c. On the bottom and side of the cereal box, draw lines connecting the front and back lines.
d. Cut out the section shown in the picture along your lines.
e. Stand the cutout section on the 3-inch (7.5-cm) side, which will be the bottom of your chariot. The open side is the back of the chariot. Mark one point 1 inch (2.5 cm) down from the top and another ½ inch (1.25 cm) in from the back on one side of the box. Draw a line connecting these points.
f. Repeat on the other side, then cut out along your lines.

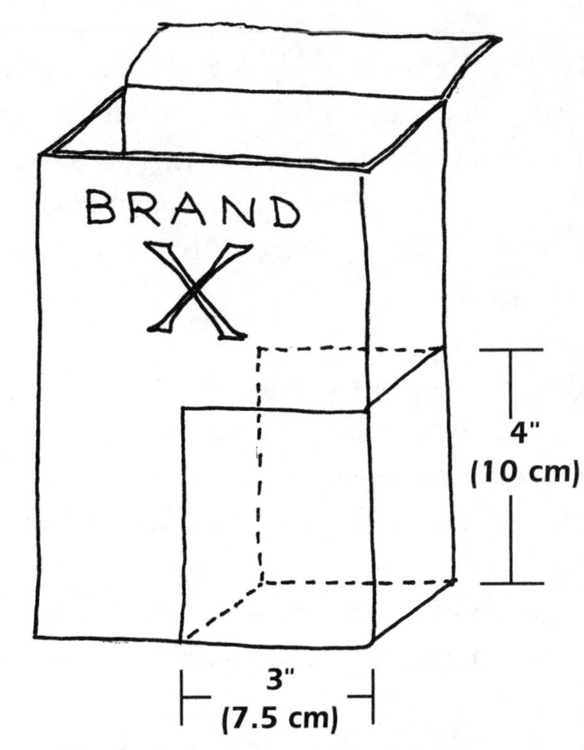

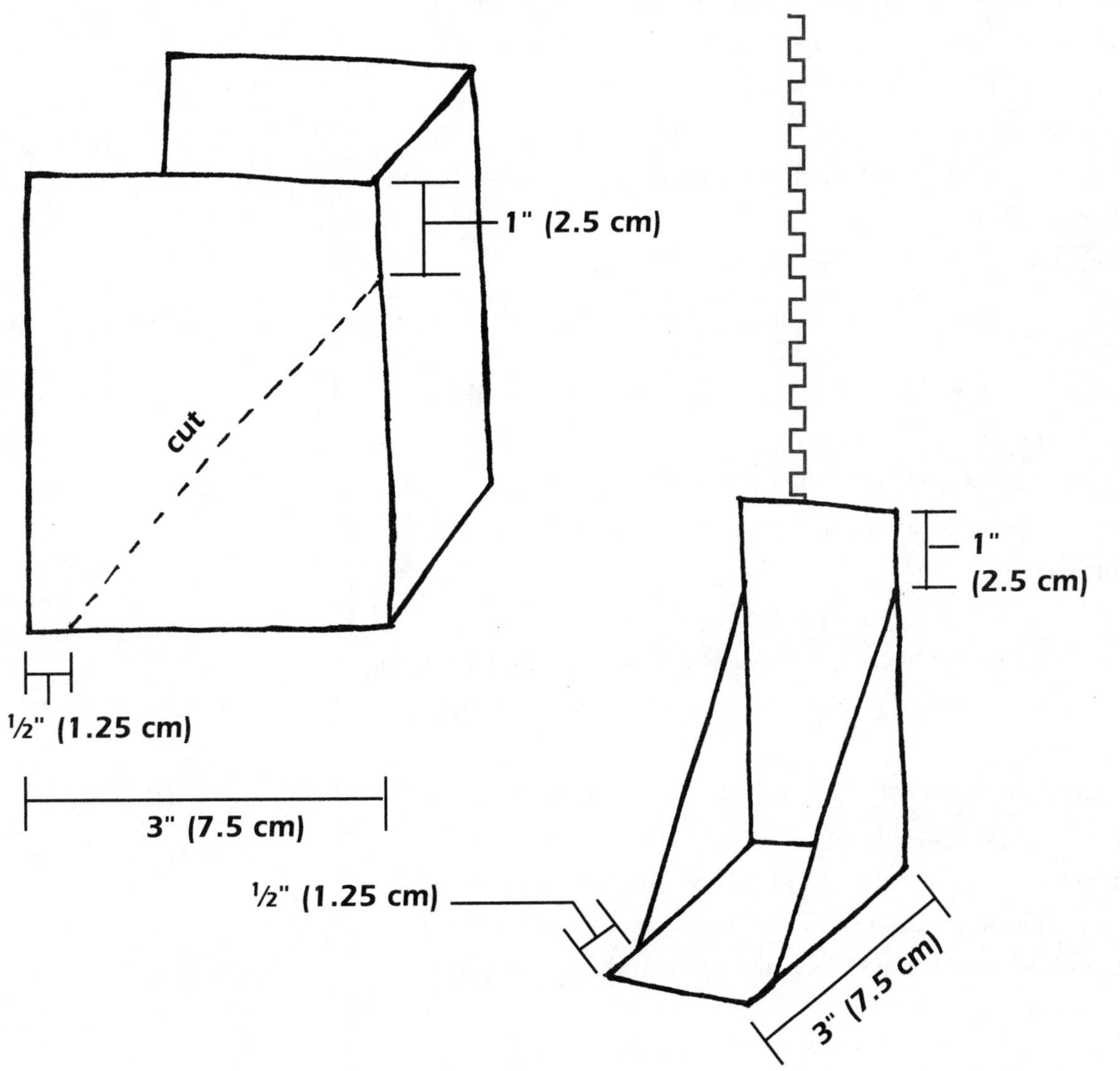

2. Turn your chariot upside down, and mark a point 1 inch (2.5 cm) back from the front edge, on either side. Draw a line on the bottom between these points. This is where the axle will go. Find the center of this line, and draw a line from it to the center front. This is where the shaft will go, as in the drawing on page 51.

3. Make the chariot's wheels.
a. Place the can on the corrugated cardboard. Draw around it twice, to make two 3-inch (7.5-cm) circles. Cut these out.
b. With the pencil and ruler, draw lines to divide each circle into quarters.
c. At the center of the circle where the lines cross, use the sharpened pencil to poke a hole the thickness of your short, unsharpened pencil.
d. With the black marker, draw the design shown here on each wheel. Cut out four triangles from each wheel as shown.

4. Make hubcaps for your wheels.
a. Cut a 1-by-½-inch (2.5-by-1.25-cm) piece from one short end of the thin cardboard.
b. Cut this piece into two ½-inch (1.25-cm) squares.

5. Make the shaft.
a. Fold the remaining thin cardboard the long way, to make a strip 4 x ½ inch (10 x 1.25 cm).
b. Put glue along the folds of the cardboard strip, to hold it together. (If you choose to use a glue gun, ask your adult helper to do this step.)

6. Attach the axle, wheels, hubcaps, and shaft to the chariot. (If you choose to use a glue gun, ask your adult helper to do the following steps.)
a. Put a drop of glue along the axle line. Place the short, unsharpened pencil on this glue line, and allow the glue to dry.
b. Slide the wheels onto the axle, making sure they turn freely. Put a drop of glue on each of the hubcaps, and place them on the axle ends so that the wheels don't fall off. Allow the glue to dry.

c. Put glue along the shaft line, and place the folded cardboard on this glue line. When the glue is dry, your chariot is ready to roll!

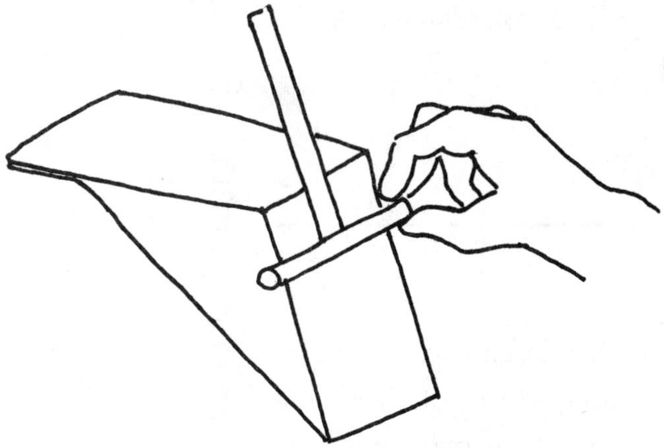

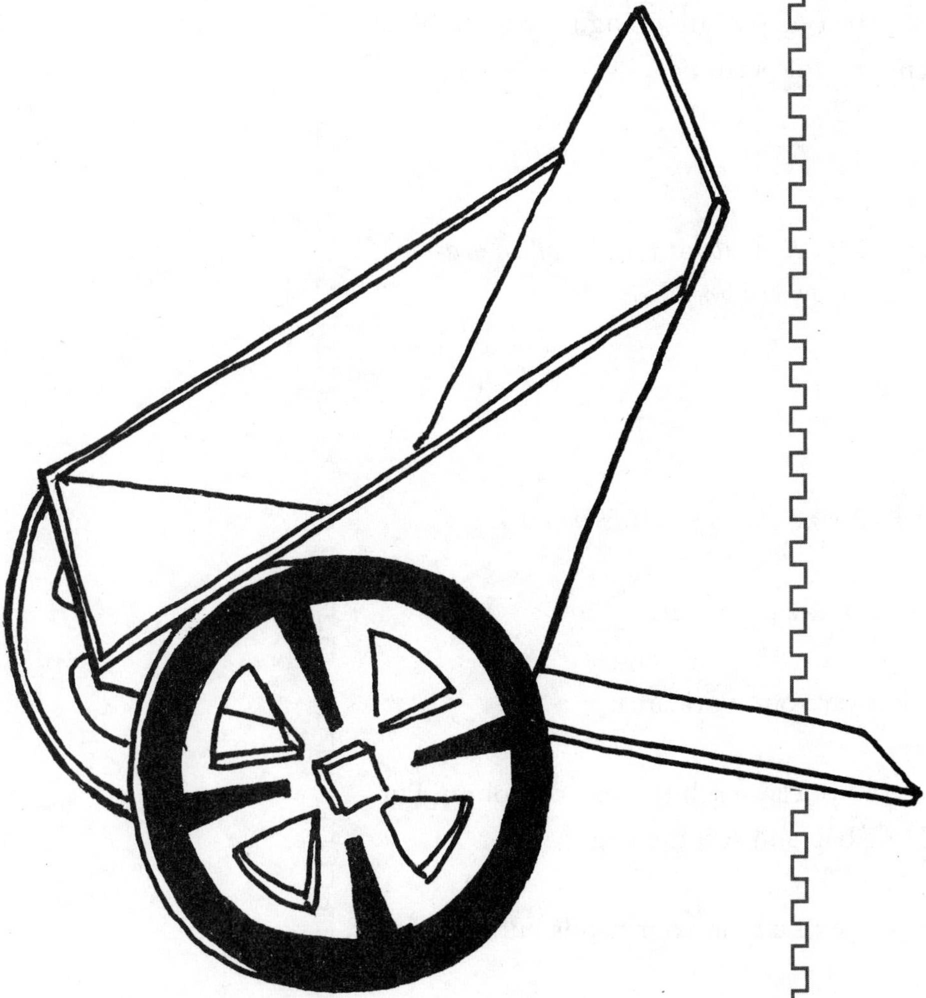

The blue chariot wins the race! The driver takes the horses away to be rubbed down, and the owner walks up to the judges to receive her prize. It is a cart full of beautiful jars, called *amphoras* (AM-fuh-ruz), filled with olive oil.

ACTIVITY

AMPHORA

The amphora was a two-handled jar with a flared neck, usually made big enough to hold about ten gallons (38 L) of olive oil. A prize amphora filled with oil was so heavy it took two men to carry it! To win one was such an honor that some athletes were buried with the amphoras they had won. The Athenians also made small amphoras like the one you are going to make. These small jars may have been used for perfume.

MATERIALS

several sheets of newspaper
1 pound (0.5 kg) self-hardening clay, about the size of an orange (Red clay is best, but any color will do.)
resealable plastic bag
craft stick or modeling tool
ruler
pencil
2 to 3 markers or pens, of varying thickness (any color)
paintbrush (optional)
red, black, and white poster paint (optional)

1. Spread the newspaper over your work area.

2. Pull off two small pieces of clay, each the size of a plum. Put these pieces into the plastic bag and seal the bag.

3. Work the remaining piece of clay in your hands until it is soft and feels warm.

4. Mold the clay into an egg shape. This will be your pot. Smooth the surface of the pot with the craft stick or your fingers to remove any holes or lines.

5. Hold the pot upright in one hand and put the index finger of your other hand on top of the clay. Push this finger through the clay almost to the bottom.

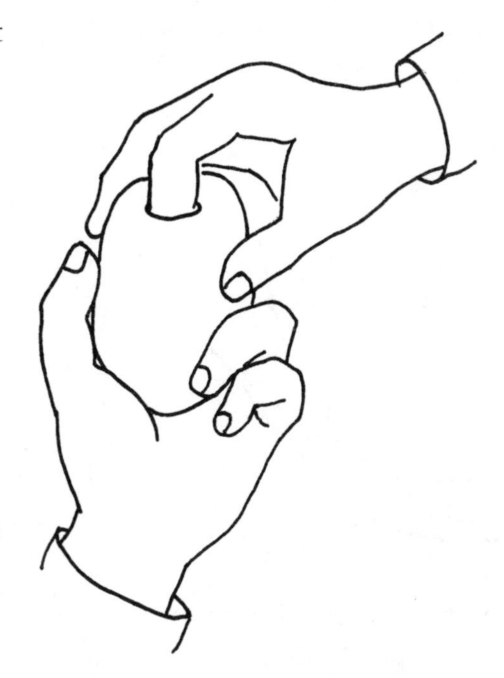

6. Holding one finger in the hole, squeeze the bottom of the pot in your other hand to make it narrower. Flatten the bottom of the pot so it can stand.

7. Holding the neck of the pot, press outward on the clay to make the shoulder flare out in a rim about 3 inches (7.5 cm)

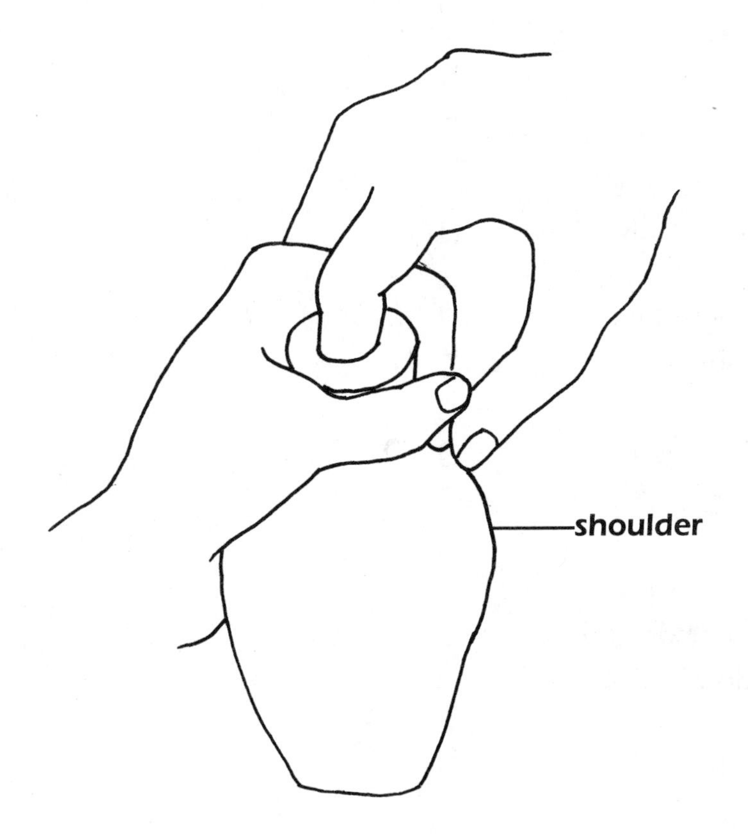

The Pots of Athens

Athens was famous for its skillful potters, who made bowls, pitchers, jars, cups, and plates to hold water, olive oil, wine, perfume, or food. The pots were made from fine red clay found near Athens. The Greek potters made pots in many different shapes for different purposes. Each kind of pot had its own name. After the potters had shaped the pots, painters decorated the pots with pictures of gods, people, animals, or other designs. Sometimes they decorated them with pictures painted in black on the red clay. On other pots they painted the background black and left the picture red. A little white paint was used for details on many pots.

8. Take one of the small pieces of clay out of the bag and flatten it with your hand to make a circle ¼ inch (0.5 cm) thick—about as thick as a pencil.

9. Stand your pot on this clay circle. Push the clay from the circle toward the bottom edge of the pot to blend the edges. Smooth with the craft stick or your fingers.

10. Take the other small piece of clay out of the bag and roll it on the newspaper until it forms a snake shape as thick as a pencil. Divide it into two equal lengths.

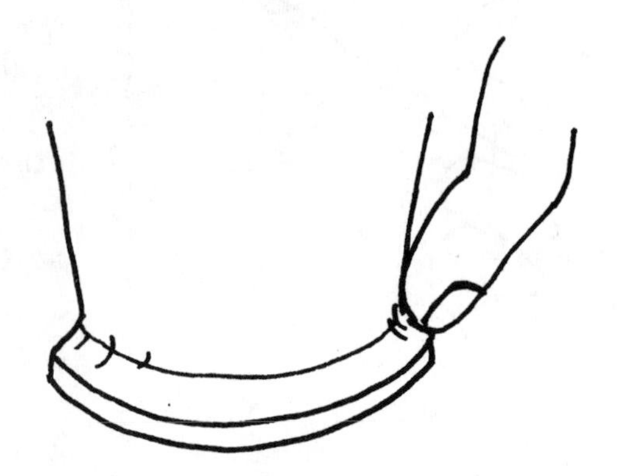

11. Take one of the snake shapes and press one end onto the rim of the pot. Press the other end onto the pot's shoulder to make a handle.

12. Repeat step 11 with the other snake shape to make a second handle.

13. Decorate your amphora.
a. Use the pencil to scratch patterns on the amphora like those shown on page 55.
b. Leave the caps on the markers or pens, and press them into the clay to make other designs.
c. Scratch your name in Greek letters into the bottom of the amphora with the pencil. (Use the Greek alphabet chart from the "Writing in Greek" activity in chapter 3.)
Note: Wash the clay off the markers and pencil as soon as you are finished.

14. Place your amphora on a piece of clean newspaper to dry. (It will leave a stain while it is wet.) Let your amphora dry for 2 days indoors, away from radiators, sunny windows, or other sources of heat.

15. (Optional) Paint your amphora when it's dry.

a. Paint the whole pot either red or black.

b. When the first coat has dried, paint over the scratched patterns in white and either red or black, whichever color you did not use for the first coat.

ACTIVITY

HYDRIA

Like all Greek pots, the large, three-handled pot called a **hydria** (HIGH-dree-uh) was made for a special purpose. Since water was not piped into people's houses, the hydria was used to carry water from a well or river. A servant like Cassandra carried the hydria on her head. The three handles made pouring easy. In this activity, you'll make a miniature version of an ancient Greek hydria.

MATERIALS

the same materials as in the previous activity

1. Make a pot as in steps 1 through 4 of the previous activity.

2. Hold the pot upright in one hand and put the index finger of your other hand on top of the clay. Push this finger through the clay almost to the bottom.

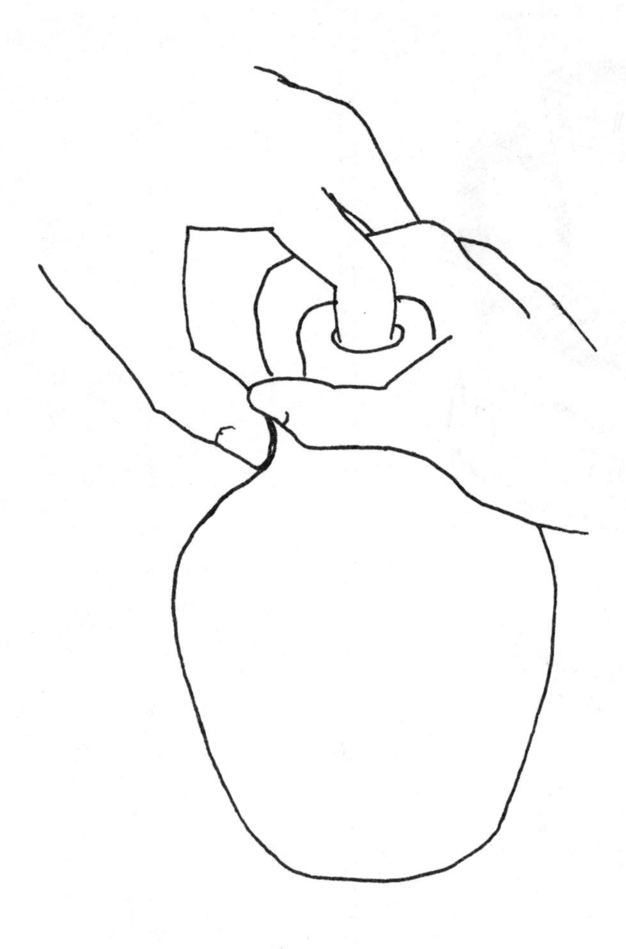

3. Holding one finger in the hole, squeeze the bottom of the pot in your other hand to make it narrower. Flatten the bottom of the pot so it can stand.

4. Holding the neck of the pot, pull outward on the clay to make a rim about 3 inches (7.5 cm) across.

5. Take one of the small pieces of clay out of the bag and flatten it with your hand to make a circle ¼ inch (0.6 cm) thick—about as thick as a pencil.

6. Stand your pot on this clay circle. Push the clay from the circle toward the bottom edge of the pot to blend the edges. Smooth with the craft stick or your fingers.

7. Take the other small piece of clay out of the bag and roll it on the newspaper until it forms a snake shape as thick as a pencil. Divide it into three equal lengths.

8. Take one of the snake shapes and press one end onto the top neck rim of the pot. Press the other end onto the pot's shoulder to make a handle.

9. Take the other two snake shapes and press them onto the pot's shoulders to make two more handles. Position each handle one-fourth of the way around from the first handle, so that these two handles are on opposite sides of the pot.

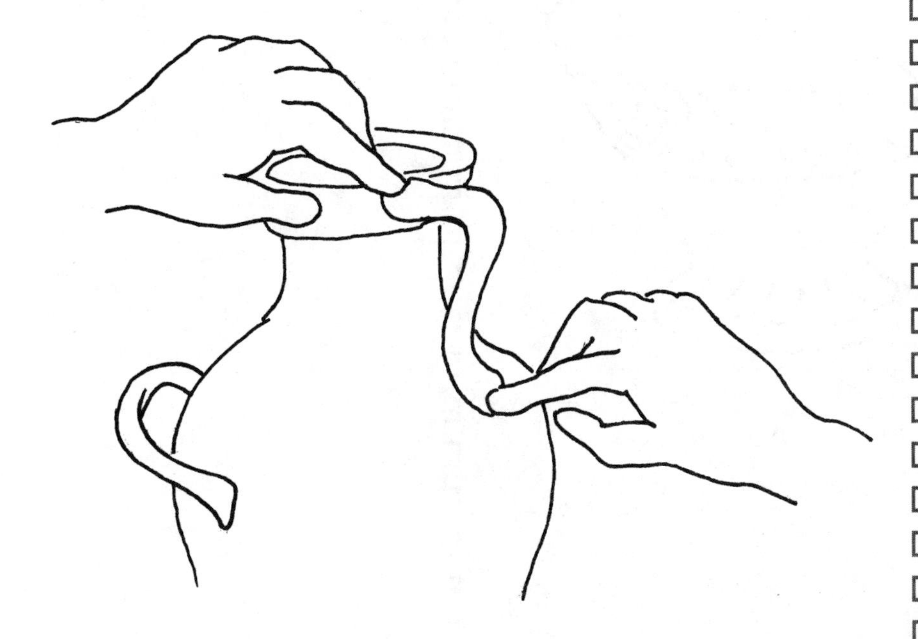

10. Decorate your hydria.

a. Use the pencil to scratch patterns on the hydria like those shown on page 58.

b. Leave the caps on the markers or pens, and press them into the clay to make other designs.

c. Scratch your name in Greek letters into the bottom of the hydria with the pencil. (Use the Greek alphabet chart from the "Writing in Greek" activity in chapter 3.)

Note: Wash the clay off the markers and pencil as soon as you are finished.

11. Place your hydria on a clean piece of newspaper to dry. (It will leave a stain while it is wet.) Let your hydria dry for 2 days indoors, away from radiators, sunny windows, or other sources of heat.

12. (Optional) Paint your hydria when it's dry.

a. Paint the whole pot either red or black.

b. When the first coat is dry, paint over the scratched patterns in either red or black, whichever color you did not use for the first coat.

c. Use white paint to color some of the patterns.

CHAPTER • 7

The Boat Race

While the pentathlon is taking place in the agora, and the chariot race is finishing at the hippodrome, about four miles (6.5 km) away another exciting event is about to begin. This is the *regatta* (rig-GAH-tuh), or boat race, which is held at Piraeus, the harbor of Athens.

Large trading ships with big square sails and rows of oars are tied up at the dock in Piraeus. On ordinary days men are always busily at work loading and unloading these ships. But today the merchants' dock is quiet. No captain is shouting orders to his sailors. No trader is calling out the price of his cargo.

Today all the noise and activity are happening at another

pier, where the boat races have just begun. Hundreds of men and boys are crowded on the pier, shouting advice and encouragement to their favorite crews.

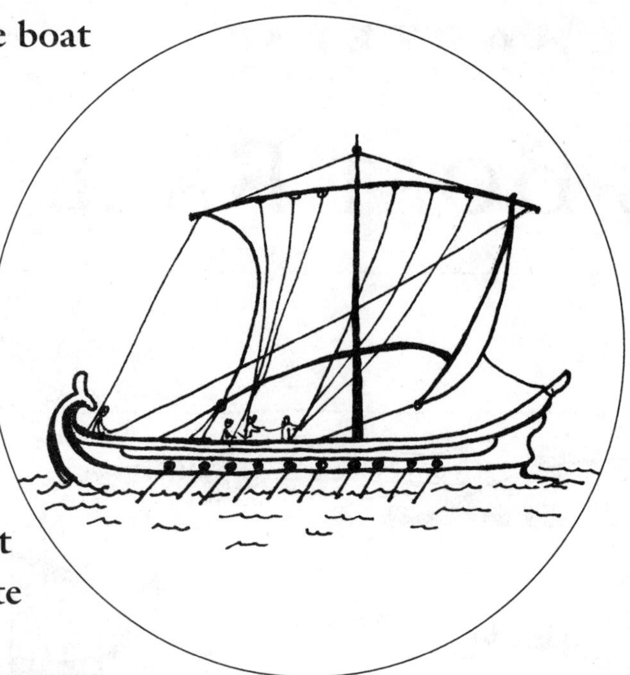

A brisk breeze blows up small waves in the sea, and seagulls swoop and squawk above the food sellers who walk through the crowd. The air smells of salt and seaweed and fresh paint—the racing boats tossing on the water have all been given a bright new coat. There are many different boat races today. Some are for small boats with only eight rowers, and others are for large boats with dozens of rowers.

ACTIVITY

GREEK BOAT

The Greeks traveled all around the Aegean and Mediterranean Seas in large ships called **triremes** (try-REEMS), or galleys. These ships were powered by big square sails and three rows of oars manned by slaves. You can build your own miniature Greek boat in this activity. Or build two, and have a boat race with a friend!

MATERIALS

pencil
5-by-1½-inch (12.5-by-3.75-cm) piece of corrugated cardboard
ruler

scissors
10-inch (25-cm) square of aluminum foil
one-hole paper punch
3-by-4-inch (7.5-by-10-cm) piece of white paper
small piece of self-hardening clay, about the size of a grape
plastic drinking straw
white glue

1. Make the bottom of the boat by drawing the oval shape shown here on the corrugated cardboard. Make the oval about 5 inches (12.5 cm) long and 1½ inches (3.75 cm) wide, with pointed ends. Cut it out.

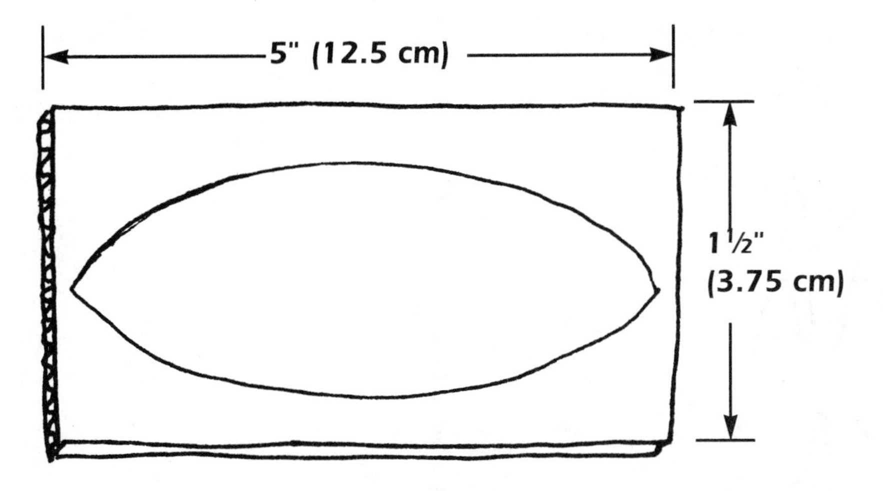

2. Make the sides of the boat.

a. Fold the foil square in half. Place the cardboard oval lengthwise in the middle of the folded foil.

b. Fold the foil over the cardboard, bringing the foil up and over to make the sides of the boat.

c. Squeeze the ends of the foil together to make the prow (front) and stern (back) of the boat.

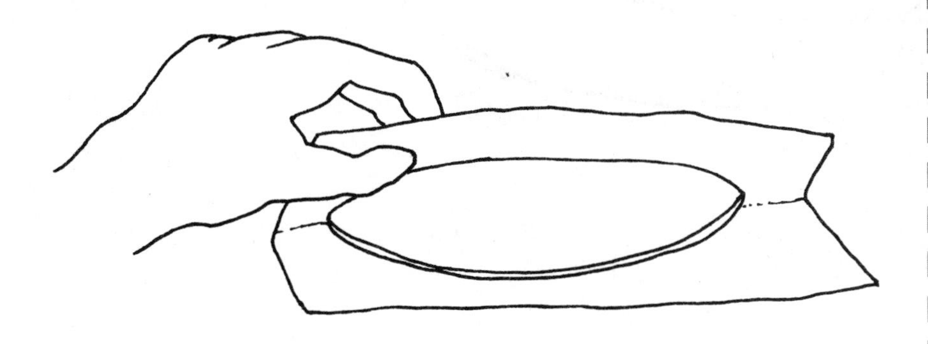

Boats and Travel

As an ancient Greek, your homeland was made up of islands and mountains. The roads were not very good, so if you needed to travel, you usually went by boat.

Like everyone else in Athens, you depended on the sea for survival. Fish was often on your dinner table. As a trader, you might grow rich by sending ships all around the Mediterranean. The powerful Athenian navy defended you.

As an Athenian girl, you learned to swim. As a boy you learned to swim, sail, and row. Because of the importance of the sea in your life, you prayed to the god of the sea, Poseidon (puh-SIE-dun), whose temple stood guard on the cliff at Sounion (SOON-ee-un) near Athens.

3. Make the sail and mast (the pole that supports the sail).
a. Punch a hole in the top center and bottom center of your paper.
b. Squeeze the piece of clay in your fingers until it feels warm. Shape it into a round disk about 1 inch (2.5 cm) in diameter and ¼ inch (0.6 cm) thick.
c. Make the mast by cutting the straw down to 6 inches (15 cm).
d. Push the straw through the holes in the paper sail.
e. Stick the straw into the clay disk so it stands, then place the sail in the center of your boat.

4. Allow the clay to dry for 2 days. When the clay is dry, put a drop of glue on the bottom of the clay disk to hold it in the boat. Now sail your boat!

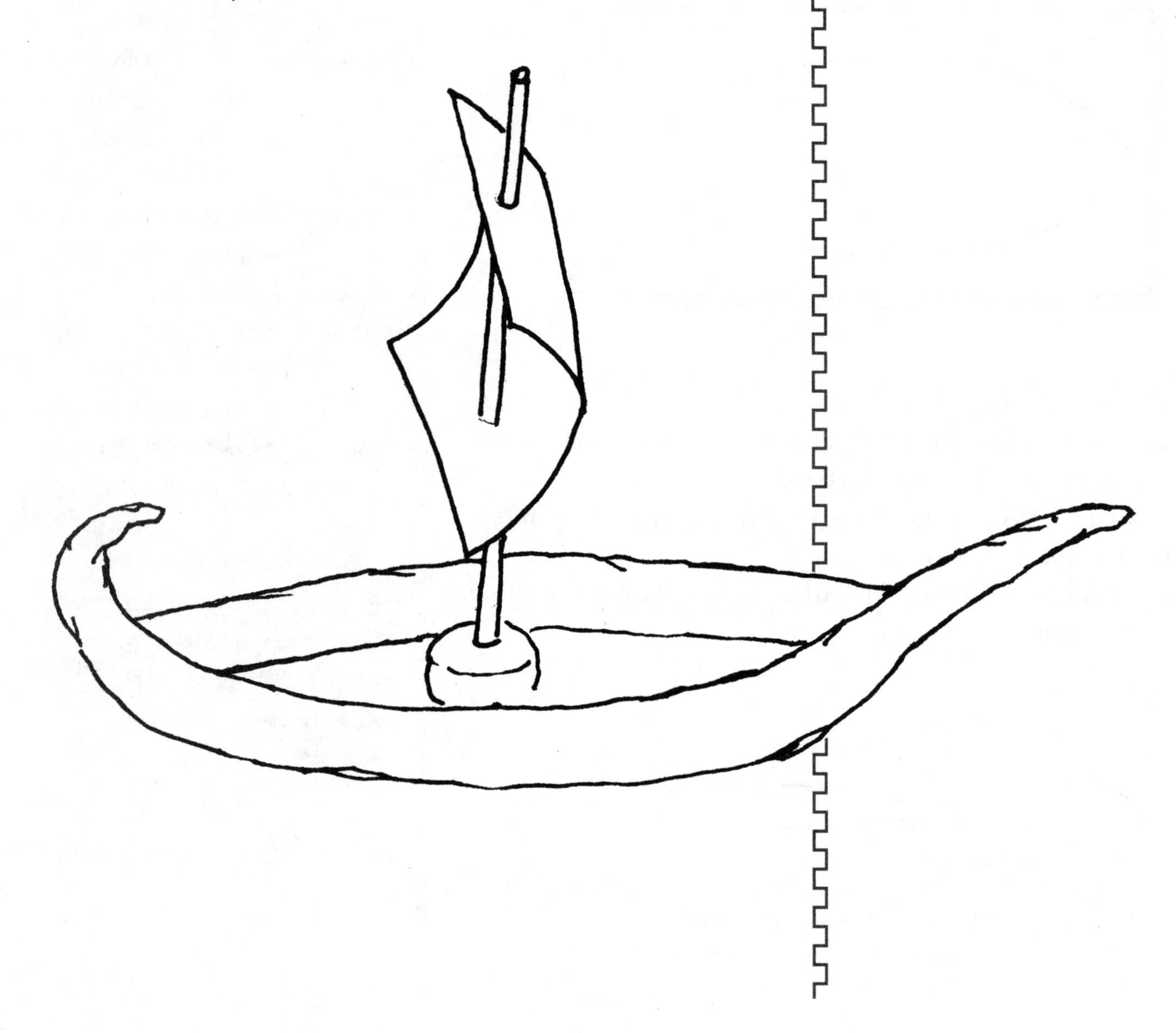

ACTIVITY

TRIDENT

Poseidon's symbol was the **trident,** a three-pronged spear used for catching fish. If you want to dress up as Poseidon, you need curly hair and a beard, and this trident!

MATERIALS

4 double sheets of newspaper
masking tape
pencil
shoe box lid
scissors
aluminum foil
transparent tape

1. Take one corner of all four sheets of newspaper and roll them up tightly. Keep rolling to the opposite corner.

2. Use several pieces of masking tape to tape the roll together tightly.

POSEIDON'S GIFT

Greek legend tells that the people of Athens were unsure whether they should make Athena or Poseidon their chief god, so they held a contest to see which of the two gods would give them the better gift. Athena planted olive trees, giving the people food and light (because they burned the oil in lamps). Poseidon struck a rock with his trident, and water sprang out.

At first the people thought that Poseidon's gift was better, until they tasted the water. Because Poseidon ruled the sea, his spring was salty and the water could not be drunk! So Athena became the chief god of Athens.

3. Copy the trident drawing shown here on the shoe box lid. Cut it out.

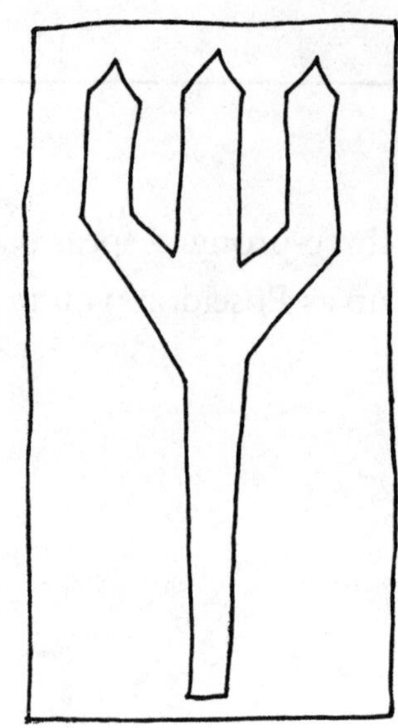

4. Insert the long end of the cardboard trident into the newspaper roll. Use masking tape to tape them together securely.

5. Cover the whole trident with aluminum foil. Tape the edges of the foil together with transparent tape.

CHAPTER • 8

THE HOPLITE RACE

After the boys' pentathlon, Philip and Alexander stay to watch a special race for armed soldiers called *hoplites* (HOP-lites). The hoplites are the best foot soldiers in the Athenian army. They run this race dressed in battle armor to show how fast they can chase the enemy.

Twenty hoplites march smartly up to the starting line. They are all young men in their twenties and look healthy and fit. The audience cheers, because Greeks admire handsome people. Brightly polished bronze helmets shine in the sun as the soldiers line up. Their helmets are decorated with horsehair plumes that blow in the wind. Bronze shin guards called *greaves* protect the soldiers'

legs. The sun sparkles on their brightly painted shields. Each hoplite carries his shield on his left arm, just as he would in battle, leaving his right arm free to hold his spear or sword.

ACTIVITY

HELMET

The Corinthian helmet was named after the Greek city-state of Corinth, because many ancient Greek helmets like this were made there. The helmet was made of bronze, which is a mixture of copper and tin. A Corinthian helmet was often decorated with a plume, a strip of horsehair or feathers that was dyed red, white, or black. You can make your helmet from a paper paint bucket and decorate it with a construction paper plume.

MATERIALS

measuring tape
5-quart (5-L) paper paint bucket
crayon (any color)
ruler
scissors
2 double sheets of newspaper
duct tape
12-by-9-inch (30-by-23-cm) piece of construction paper, either red, white, or black
pencil
helper

1. Make the face of the helmet.

a. Use the measuring tape to measure two points on the rim of the bucket 4 inches (10 cm) apart. Use the crayon to mark them A and B.

b. With your fingers on these marks, put on the bucket so that marks A and B are at the corners of your mouth.

c. With the bucket on, have your helper use the crayon to make marks on the bucket at the tip of your nose and at your eyes.

d. Take the bucket off.

e. Using the crayon, copy the design here by drawing up from marks A and B to just below the marks for your eyes. Draw around the eye and nose areas as shown, leaving a strip about 1½ inches (3.75 cm) wide to cover your nose.

f. Use the scissors to cut out along your lines.

2. Make the top, back, and sides of the helmet.

a. Crumple the newspaper into a ball and place it on top of the helmet.

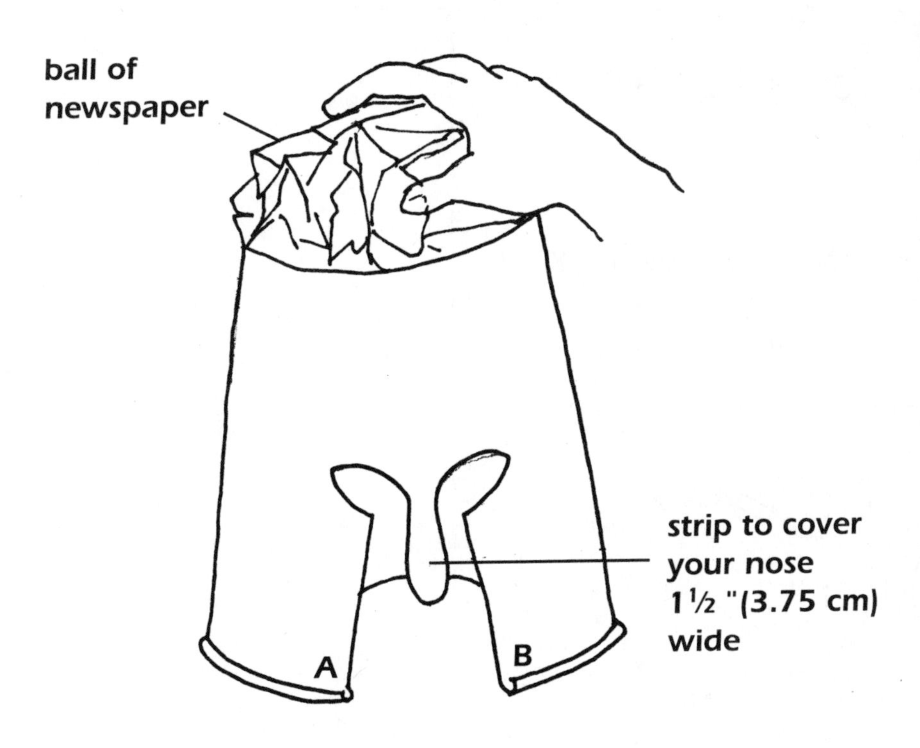

b. Cut the duct tape in 15 strips 14 inches (35 cm) long.

c. Use the strips to tape the ball of newspaper to the helmet.

d. Cut 15 more strips of duct tape 14 inches (35 cm) long.

SOLDIERS

As a boy in Athens, you were drafted into the army at age eighteen for two years military training Growing up in Athens, you believed that military service was just one of your adult responsibilities. You also looked forward to making a career to support your family, taking part in politics, enjoying sports, and discussions with friends.

But as a boy and man in Sparta, Athen's great rival among the Greek city-states, you considered military service the most important part of life. In Sparta, when you were born, the leaders inspected you to see if you were healthy enough to serve in the army when you grew up. If you weren't, you were left outside to die. If you passed this test, you lived at home until you were seven, when you were taken from your home and sent to military school.

e. Tape these strips from the rim to the top of the helmet, overlapping them slightly, until the entire helmet is covered. Tape around the edges of the face area.

3. Make the plume.

a. Fold the construction paper in half lengthwise.

b. With the pencil and ruler, draw a line across the folded paper ½ inch (1.25 cm) in from the fold.

c. Keeping the paper folded and beginning ½ inch (1.25 cm) in from the end, cut through both layers from the edges of the paper to the line you drew. Continue to make cuts ½ inch (1.25 cm) apart all along the paper.

d. Fold the paper along the line you drew as shown.

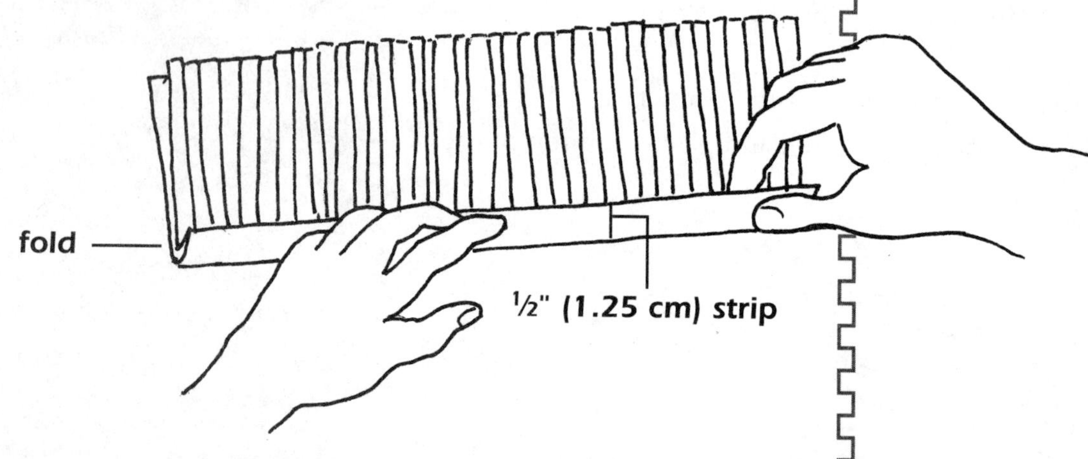

e. Glue the folded edge of the paper to the helmet, starting 8 inches (20 cm) above the tip of the nose.

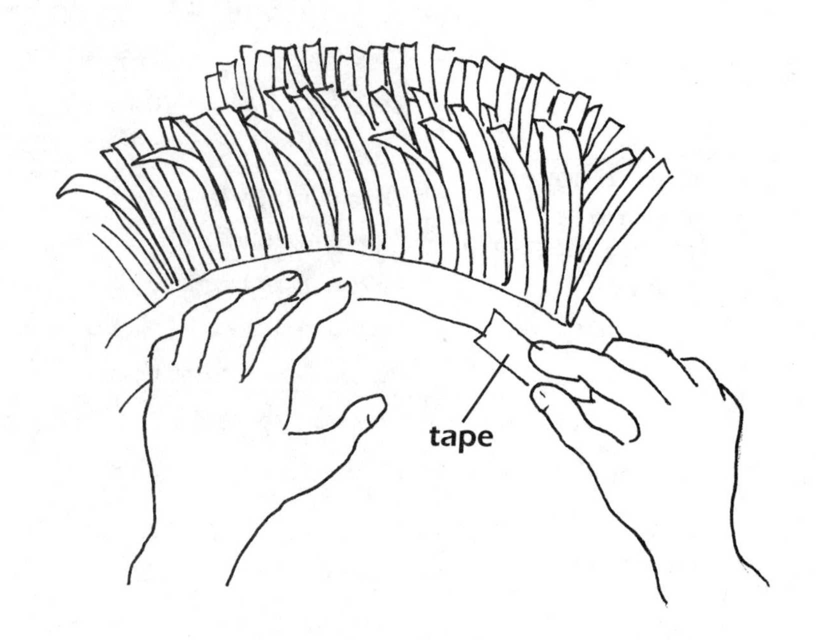

4. Let the glue dry, and your helmet is ready.

At the end of the hoplite race, the audience rises up to cheer for the young soldiers. They are not even out of breath after running two lengths of the track! When the winner has received his prize, the hoplites line up and march out together. Alexander can hardly wait to join the army and wear armor like theirs! He and Philip follow the soldiers out of the agora and head for home.

ACTIVITY

GREAVES

Greaves were bronze shin guards that were tied on with leather straps and worn in battle. They were often decorated with a pattern like the one shown on the next page. Make your own greaves from cardboard or poster board.

MATERIALS

scissors
ruler

THE FIRST MARATHON

The first **marathon** was run after the Athenian army won an important battle against the Persians at Marathon in 490 B.C. When the battle ended, a messenger ran all the way to Athens, about twenty miles (32 km) away, to report the news. As soon as he had announced the victory, he fell dead.

The first modern marathon was run at the Olympic Games in 1896. The modern marathon is a long-distance race, twenty-six miles and 385 yards (4.2 km) long.

pencil with eraser
20-by-15-inch (50-by-37-cm) piece of brown or gray cardboard or poster board
black marker
one-hole paper punch
40-inch (100-cm) piece of string

1. Cut the cardboard in half to make two pieces, each 15 x 10 inches (37.5 x 25 cm). Set one piece aside.

2. Make one greave.
a. Take one piece of cardboard and use the ruler to find the center point (5 inches or 12.5 cm) on one short side. Use the pencil to mark this point A. This will be the top end of the greave.
b. Find the center point at the opposite end of the cardboard. Mark this point B.
c. From point B, measure 1¾ inches (4.5 cm) on each side and 1 inch (2.5 cm) up from the bottom, and mark these points X.

3. Along each long side of cardboard, measure 5 inches (12.5 cm) down from the top of the greave and 1 inch (2.5 cm) in from the sides. Mark these points Y.

4. Use the ruler and pencil to draw a straight line connecting points X and Y on each side. Draw curved lines from point Y up to point A on each side. Cut out along the lines you drew.

5. With the pencil, copy the design shown here. Go over your drawing in black marker.

6. Punch holes at points X and Y. Cut four pieces of string each 10 inches (25 cm) long. Tie a string to each hole.

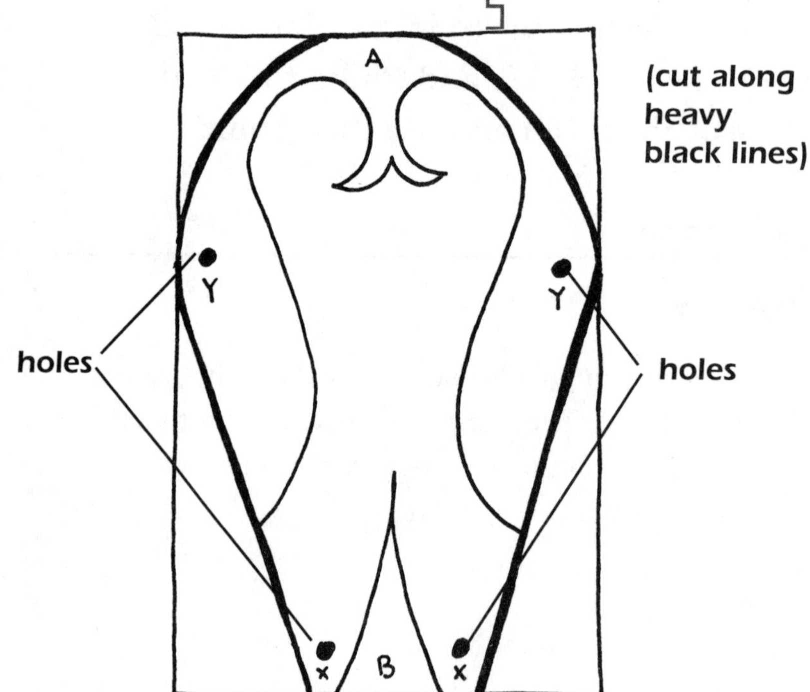

7. Erase all pencil marks.

8. Take the second cardboard half from step 1. Repeat steps 2 through 7 to make the second greave.

9. Tie the greaves to your shins as shown.

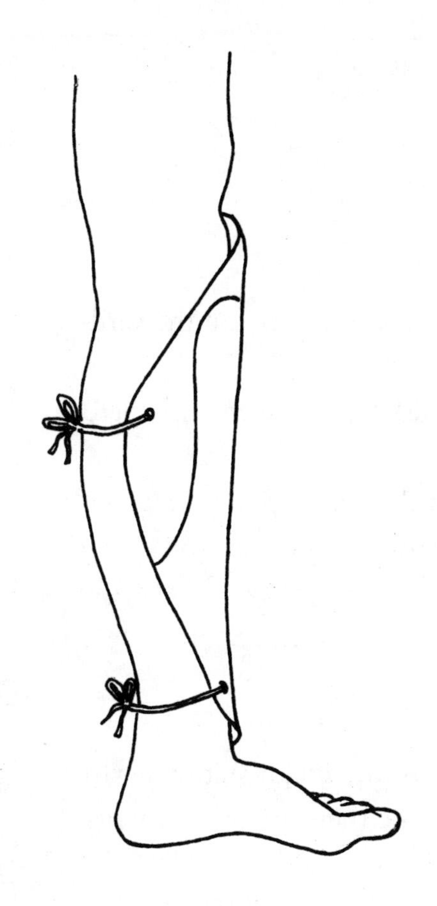

ACTIVITY

SHIELD

Greek soldiers carried shields made of wood and leather. These were decorated with painted designs showing people, animals, or monsters. The designs made it easy to tell one soldier from another. The picture here shows a Greek monster called a Gorgon. The **Gorgons** were three hideous sisters—Medusa (meh-DOO-sah), Euryale (yoo-RYE-al-ee), and Stheno (sth-EE-no)—who had snakes for hair. They were thought to be so ugly that they drove people mad! You can copy the picture here on your shield or make your own design.

MATERIALS

ruler
pencil
24-inch (60-cm) square piece of corrugated cardboard
drawing compass
scissors
12-by-½-inch (30-by-1.25-cm) piece of sewing elastic or cardboard

4 brass fasteners
masking tape
colored markers
adult helper

1. Make the shield.
a. Use the ruler and pencil to draw a diagonal line on the cardboard square from corner to corner.
b. Repeat with the other corners. Mark the center point where the lines cross.
c. Place the point of the compass on the center point. Use the compass to draw a circle on the cardboard 24 inches (60 cm) in diameter.
d. Use the scissors to cut out your circular shield.

2. Make the arm straps.
a. Place your forearm on the center of the shield. With your free hand, mark a dot on the cardboard on either side of your wrist and forearm.
b. Ask your adult helper to use the pointed end of the compass to make holes through each dot you marked.
c. Cut the strip of elastic into two pieces, one 7 inches (17.5 cm) long and the other 5 inches (12.5 cm) long.
d. Ask the adult to use the pointed end of the compass to make a hole in each end of the two strips.

3. Fasten the arm straps on the shield.
a. Lift up the shield and hold the shorter elastic strip against the cardboard where your wrist goes.
b. From the opposite side of the cardboard, push each fastener through the hole in the cardboard and the hole in the elastic.
c. Open the ends of the fasteners to fasten the elastic as shown.
d. Repeat steps 3a through 3c to fasten the longer elastic strip where your forearm goes.

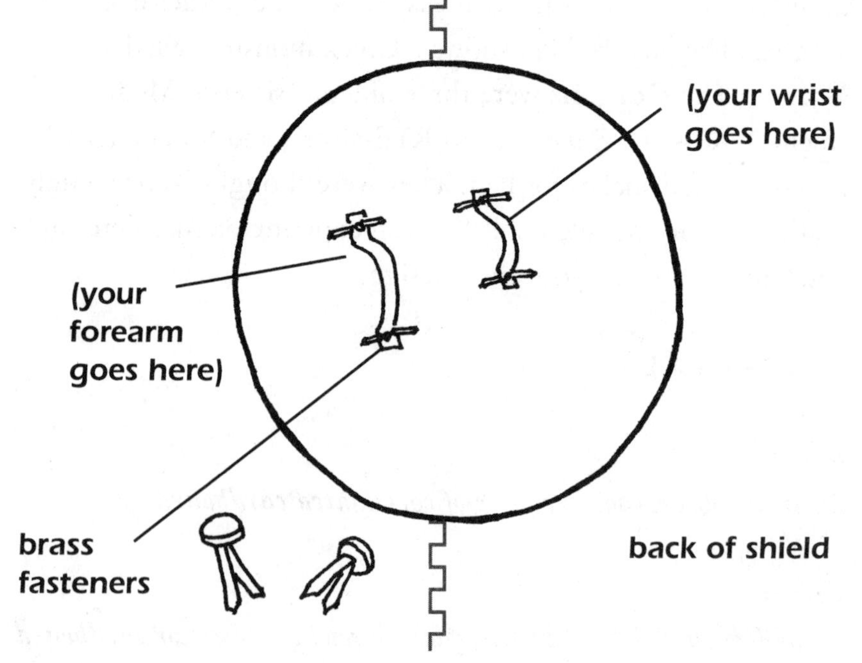

e. Turn the shield over and cover the ends of the fasteners with masking tape.

4. Now draw the design shown on the shield in pencil. Use markers to color in the design.

Shield design (Gorgon head)

ALEXANDER THE GREAT

One of the most famous ancient Greek soldiers was Alexander the Great. He was born a prince in the Greek city-state of Macedonia in 356 B.C. He was educated by the great philosopher Aristotle and became king at the age of twenty.

Alexander led his army to victory over the Persian Empire. He expanded Greek rule all the way across India, but died at the age of thirty-two, before he could establish a lasting peace.

CHAPTER • 9

Getting Ready for the Parade

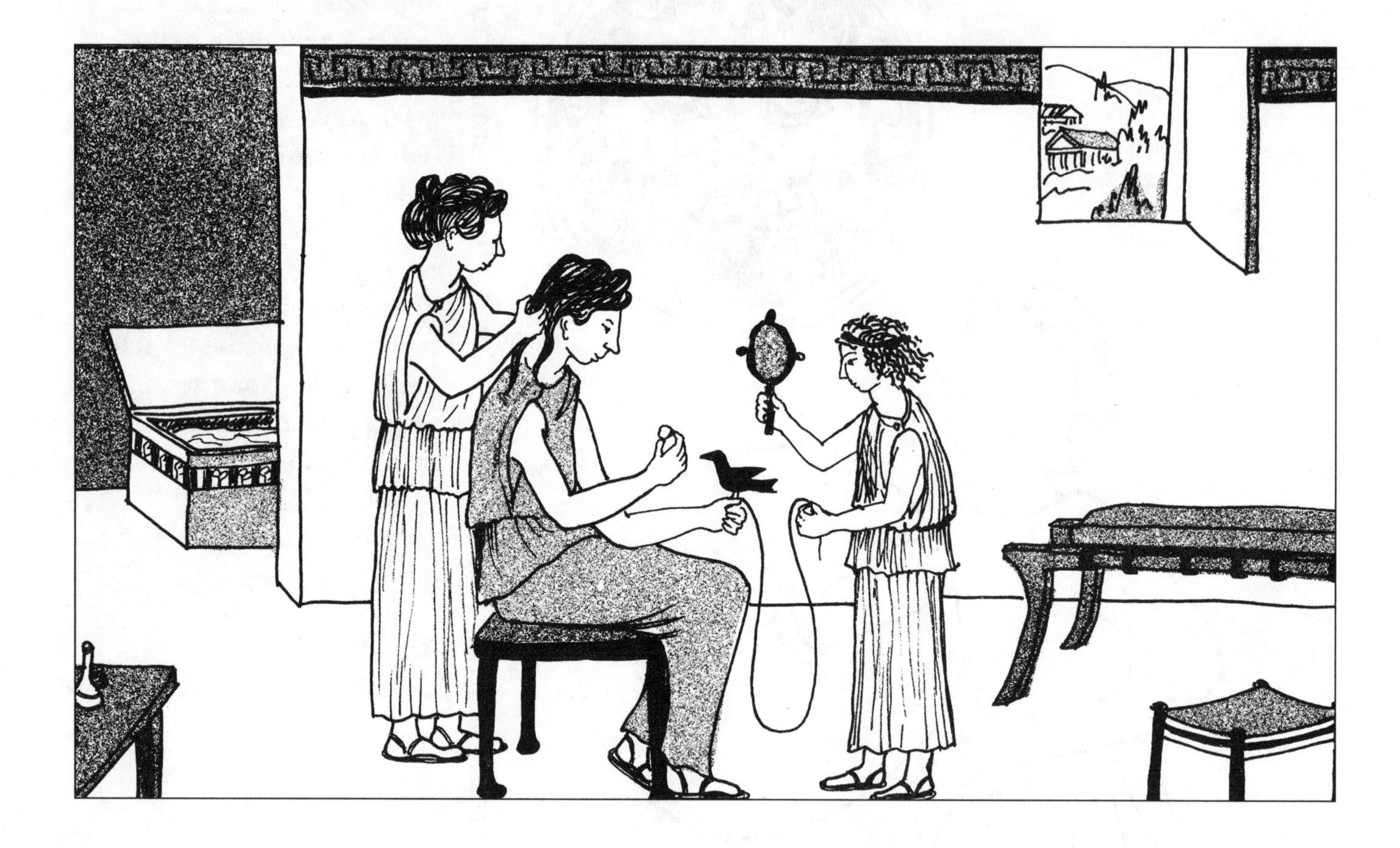

After the hoplite race, Philip and Alexander walk home through the market. They stop at a jewelry stall to buy a gift for Helen in honor of her birthday next week. Philip asks Alexander to pick whatever he thinks Helen would like best. Alexander enjoys shopping. He looks carefully at all the jewelry, and then chooses a snake bracelet, just like the one Helen's friend Aphrodite wears.

ACTIVITY

SNAKE BRACELET

To make your snake bracelet look like real gold, use gold foil from a florist shop. If you can't find gold foil, use aluminum foil and pretend it's silver. You'll also need florist's wire, which is thin wire covered with paper or plastic. It can be found at garden shops. If you can't find florist's wire, any thin metal wire will do.

MATERIALS

45-inch (112.5-cm) piece of florist's wire or any thin wire
ruler
3-by-25-inch (7.5-by-62.5-cm) piece of gold foil, not plasticized (If you can't find foil this size, use 2 shorter pieces.)

1. Fold the wire in half so it is 22½ inches (56.25 cm) long and about ½ inch (1.25 cm) wide.

2. Spread out the foil. Place the wire lengthwise on the foil ½ inch (1.25 cm) from the top and side of the foil as shown on page 76.

JEWELRY

As a Greek girl or woman, you preferred the warm shine of gold jewelry to the sparkle of colored stones. You wore rings, earrings, necklaces, bracelets, and headbands made with raised designs beaten into gold.

When people died, you buried their jewelry with them. You believed that souls lived on forever, so you thought that the dead would continue to enjoy their jewelry in the afterlife.

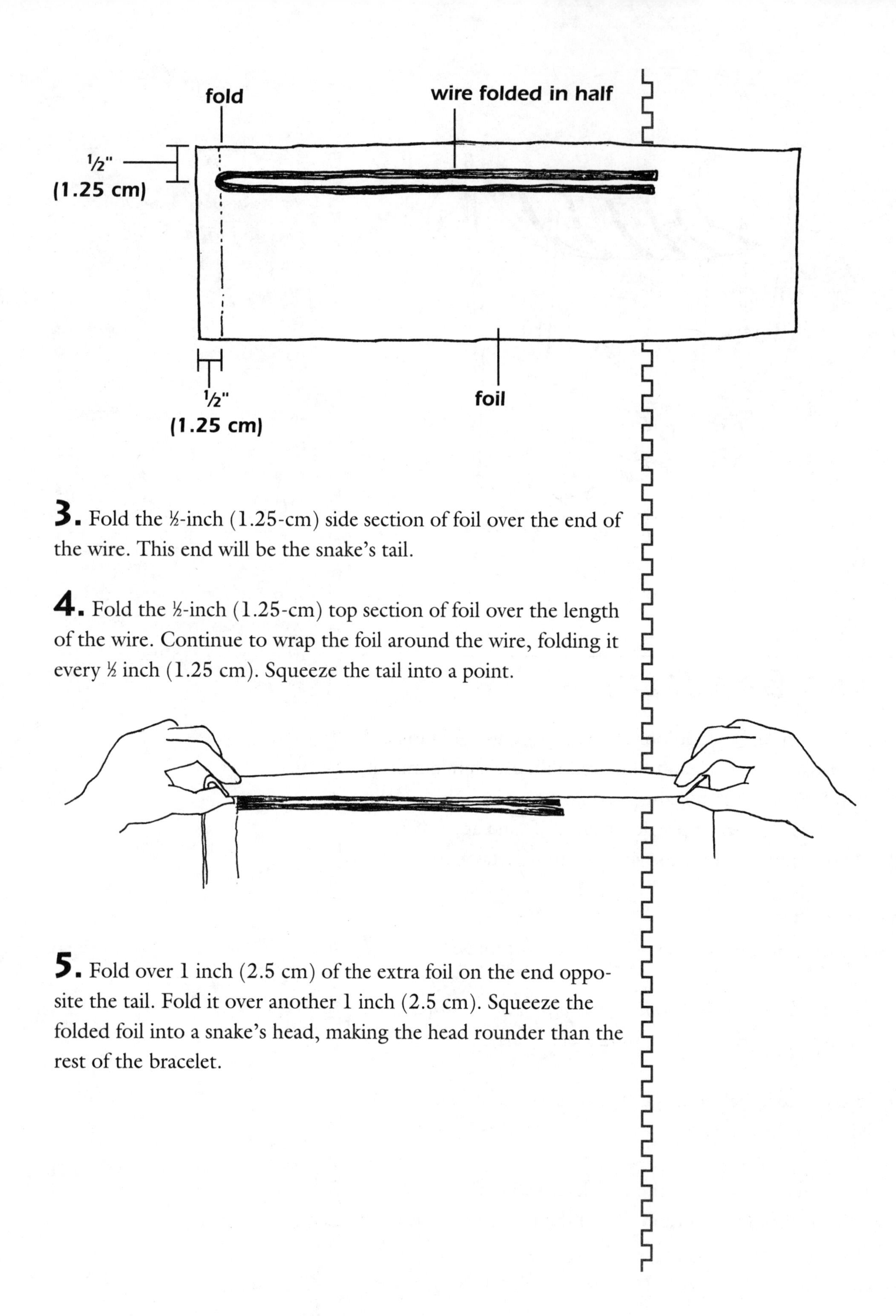

3. Fold the ½-inch (1.25-cm) side section of foil over the end of the wire. This end will be the snake's tail.

4. Fold the ½-inch (1.25-cm) top section of foil over the length of the wire. Continue to wrap the foil around the wire, folding it every ½ inch (1.25 cm). Squeeze the tail into a point.

5. Fold over 1 inch (2.5 cm) of the extra foil on the end opposite the tail. Fold it over another 1 inch (2.5 cm). Squeeze the folded foil into a snake's head, making the head rounder than the rest of the bracelet.

6. Wrap the bracelet around your arm in a spiral.

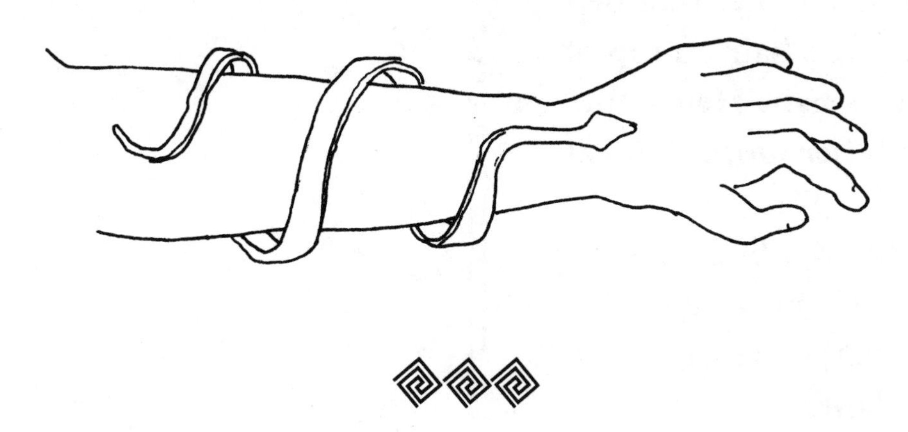

While Philip and Alexander were at the agora, Penelope and Helen have been putting the finishing touches to Athena's peplos. They finish the weaving and take it down from the loom.

Even Helen, who always worries about her work, thinks it looks beautiful. Penelope and Cassandra fold the peplos carefully for its journey to the temple on top of the Acropolis, and give it to Myron to hold.

Helen, Penelope, and Cassandra all get ready for the evening's feast. Today's dinner will be one of the year's best, and all the food must be packed in baskets, along with the dishes, knives, and spoons they will need. The meat will be given to them by the priests after the sacrifice to Athena, but everything else must come from home.

When the feast is packed, they get themselves ready. Helen washes, then dresses in her best peplos. Cassandra arranges Penelope's hair on top of her head, and then fixes Helen's hair. Helen puts on her necklace and goes to watch her mother finish getting ready.

Cassandra brings Penelope's jewel box, and they all look inside to help her choose the jewelry she will wear. They choose a bracelet, earrings, and a beautiful necklace with a pendant.

ACTIVITY

NECKLACE

Your necklace will have "gold" beads and a pendant hanging from it. To make it look real, use gold foil from a florist shop and metallic gold cord from a craft shop. If these materials aren't available, you can use aluminum foil and yellow cord.

MATERIALS

8-by-5½-inch (20-by-13.75-cm) piece of gold foil, not plasticized
ruler
8 plastic beads—2 small, 4 medium, 2 large (Beads should have a large hole for threading and a raised pattern on them.)
pencil
scissors
2-by-1¼-inch (5-by-3-cm) piece of thin, noncorrugated cardboard
felt-tip pen with flat ends
24-inch (60-cm) piece of metallic gold cord
transparent tape
small paper clip

1. Make a gold bead.
a. Tear off a piece of foil approximately 1½ x 2 inches (3.75 x 5 cm).

b. Place a bead at one end of the foil and wrap it, pressing tightly so that the bead's pattern shows.
c. With the pencil, poke through the foil at the holes in the bead.

2. Repeat step 1 with additional foil for all eight beads.

3. Make the pendant.
a. Cut a piece of foil 5 x 2½ inches (12.5 x 6.25 cm). Place the cardboard on the center of the foil.
b. Fold in the sides of the foil tightly along the edge of the cardboard.
c. Fold the bottom of the foil up over the card (fold 1 in the drawing).
d. Fold the top piece of foil in half (fold 2), then fold it down (fold 3) to make a flap as shown.

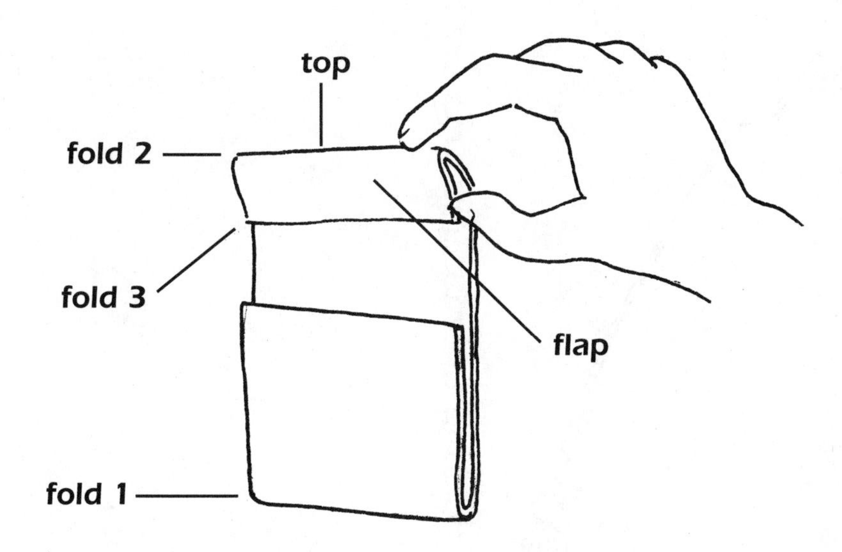

4. Decorate the pendant.
a. Use the pencil point to press a straight line in the foil all around the front of the pendant, ¼ inch (0.5 cm) in from the edge.
b. With the end of the felt-tip pen, press three circles in the foil inside your line.

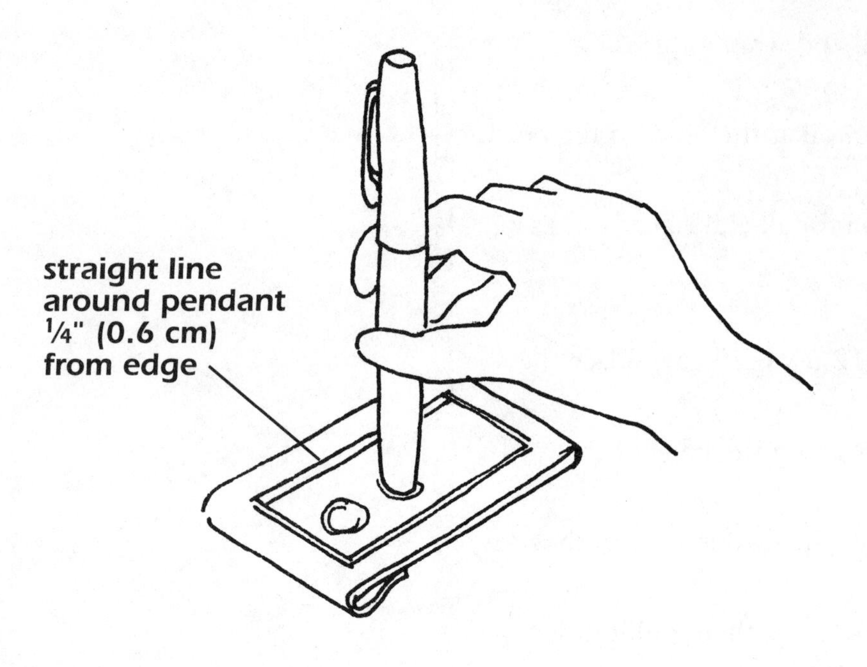

5. Assemble the necklace.

a. Place the flap of the pendant over the cord and tape it shut.

b. String four beads on the cord on one side of the pendant. Start with a large one, then two medium ones, and a small one.

c. Tie a knot at the end of the cord, making a loop as shown.

d. Repeat steps 5b and 5c on the other side of the pendant.

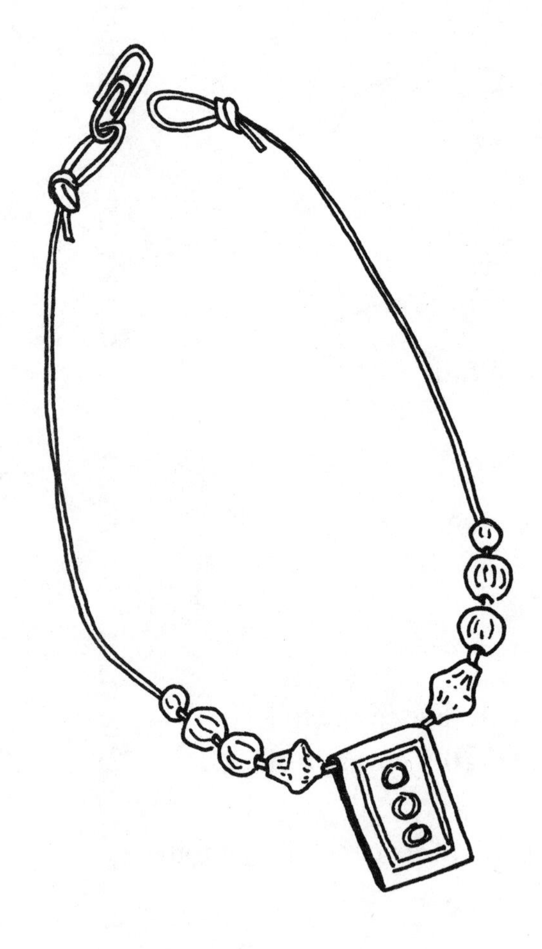

6. To fasten the necklace, hook a paper clip in the loops as shown.

ACTIVITY

EARRINGS

For the best effect, make your earrings with metallic gold cord and gold tinsel stems, which you can find at a craft shop, and gold foil from a florist shop. If these materials aren't available, you can substitute yellow cord, yellow pipe cleaners, and aluminum foil.

MATERIALS

scissors
50-inch (125-cm) piece of metallic gold cord
ruler
two 10-inch (25-cm) gold tinsel stems
6-inch (15-cm) square of gold foil, not plasticized
10 plastic beads—4 small and 6 large (available at craft stores)
pencil

1. Cut the cord in half. Set one half aside.

2. Cut one of the cord halves into 4 pieces: 9 inches (23 cm), 6 inches (15 cm), 5 inches (12 cm), and 5 inches (12 cm).

3. Tie the ends of the 9-inch (23-cm) cord together to make a loop.

4. Drape one of the tinsel stems over the cord loop.
a. Bend about ¼ inch (0.6 cm) of one end of the tinsel over the cord loop and twist to attach the tinsel to the cord.
b. Drape the tinsel from the cord to make a dip about 1¼ inches (3 cm) deep.
c. Bring the tinsel over the cord to make another dip approximately the same size.
d. Make a third dip 1½ inches (3.75 cm) deep, then bend the remaining ¼ inch (0.6 cm) of tinsel over the cord and twist to attach it to the cord.

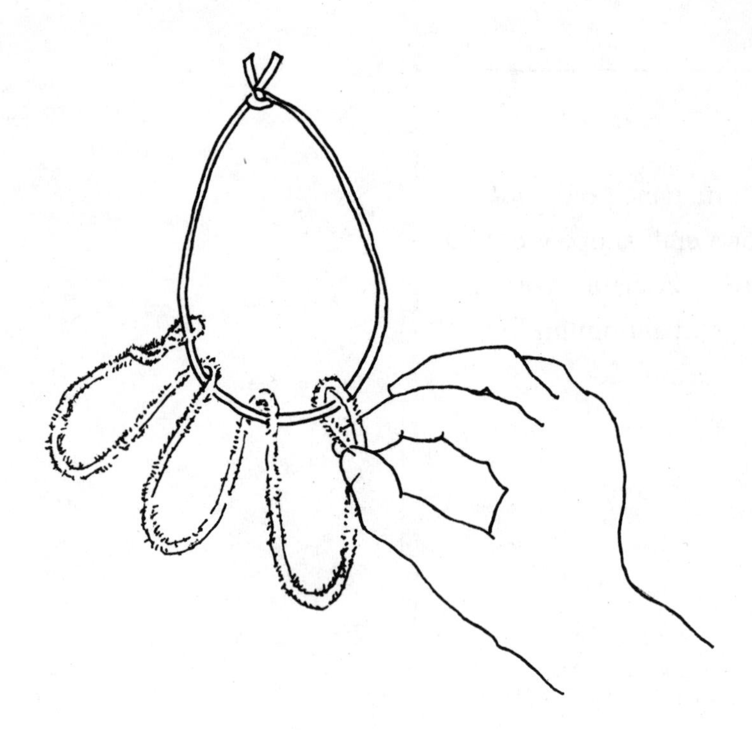

5. Cover a large bead in gold foil.
a. Tear off a piece of foil approximately 1½ x 2 inches (3.75 x 5 cm).
b. Place a large bead at one end of the foil and wrap it around the bead. Press the foil tightly so that the bead's pattern shows.
c. Use the pencil to poke through the foil at the holes in the bead.

6. Repeat step 5 with two more large beads and two small beads.

7. Tie a double knot at one end of the 6-inch (15-cm) piece of cord. Slide on one small bead, one large bead, and one small bead.

8. Tie the free end of the cord to the center of the middle tinsel section.

9. Tie a double knot at one end of one of the 5-inch (12-cm) pieces of cord. Slide a large bead on the cord.

10. Tie the free end of the cord to the center of one of the outer tinsel sections.

11. Repeat step 9 with the other 5-inch (12-cm) cord and tie it to the remaining tinsel section.

12. Take the remaining half of the original gold cord and repeat steps 2 through 9 for the other earring. Hang both over your ears when finished.

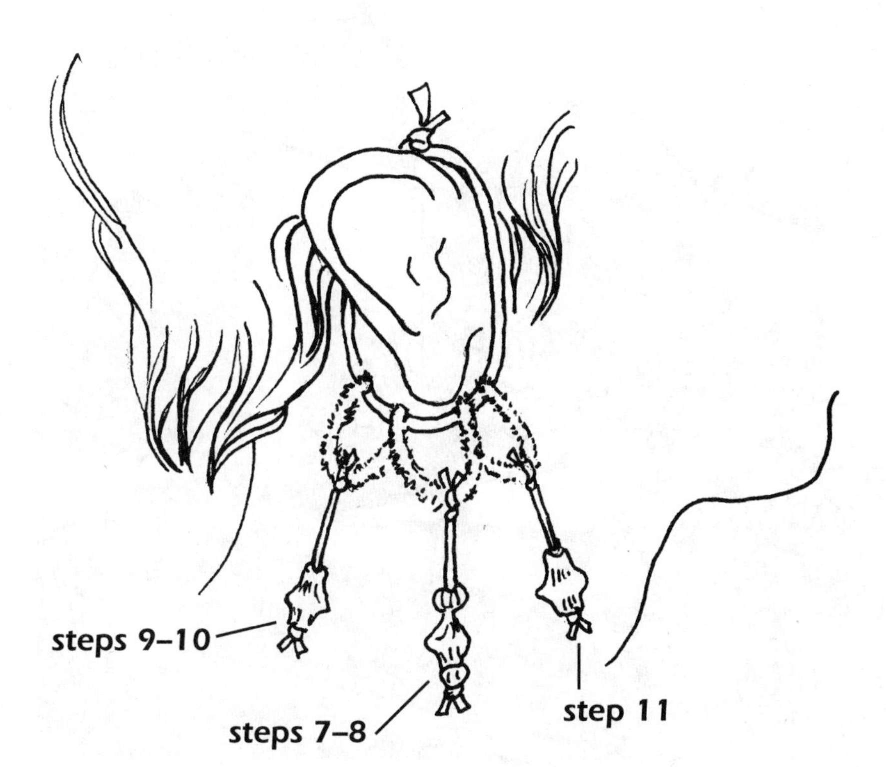

CHAPTER • 10

THE GREAT PARADE

Philip and Alexander arrive home just as Penelope and Helen have finished getting ready. Penelope and Helen take the peplos from Myron. The whole family, along with Cassandra and Myron, set off for the parade.

Nearly everyone in Athens gathers at the Dipylon (DIP-ee-lun) Gate in the northwestern corner of the city walls. Flutes and lyres start to play, and the parade moves off! It is late afternoon, and the sun is comfortably low in the sky. Thousands of people of all ages make their way across the city and up the steep path to the top of the Acropolis, crowned with its many beautiful temples.

ACTIVITY

Greek Revival Game

Architects in ancient Greece used three different styles for their buildings, just as modern architects might build a house in modern, colonial, or ranch style. The **Doric** style was the oldest, and was named for the region called Doris in central Greece. The **Ionic** style was named for the Ionian islands (in modern Turkey). The **Corinthian** style was named for the city-state of Corinth.

People all over the world copy the buildings of the ancient Greeks. These copies are called **Greek Revival** style. Architects often design important buildings, such as churches, temples, courthouses, and colleges, in Greek Revival style. Some houses are built in this style, too. Wherever you live, you can probably find buildings that copy the Greek styles.

MATERIALS

city, town, or a picture book of a city or town
Greek Revival architecture picture

Buildings

As a a girl or boy in ancient Greece, your city streets were lined with small houses and shops. If you looked high above these plain private houses, you could see many beautiful stone temples and other public buildings. These buildings had pitched roofs and porches resting on pillars called columns.

Wonderful carved stone figures decorated some temples, showing gods and heroes as large as life or bigger. These were all painted in bright colors. They looked so lifelike that as a small child you thought they were alive!

pencil
pad of paper
2 or more players

1. Next time you are walking in a city or town, see how many Greek Revival buildings you find. Or play at home, looking in a picture book of cities.

2. To recognize a Greek Revival building, look at the drawings here and search for these clues.

a. *Columns.* These are pillars that support the roof, usually across the front of the building although they may even be all around it. Check the pictures here to decide if the columns you find are Doric, Ionic, or Corinthian.

- *Doric columns.* These are the simplest style, with a fat, fluted column headed by a simple square **capital,** which is the top part of the column on which the roof rests. **Flutes** are ridges running down the side of a column.
- *Ionic columns.* These are slender, with capitals carved in hornlike curls called **volutes.**
- *Corinthian columns.* These have the fanciest capitals, carved with marvelous twisting leaves.

b. *Pediment.* The **pediment** is a triangular area at the front and back of the building, high up under the roof. It sometimes has carving or writing on it.

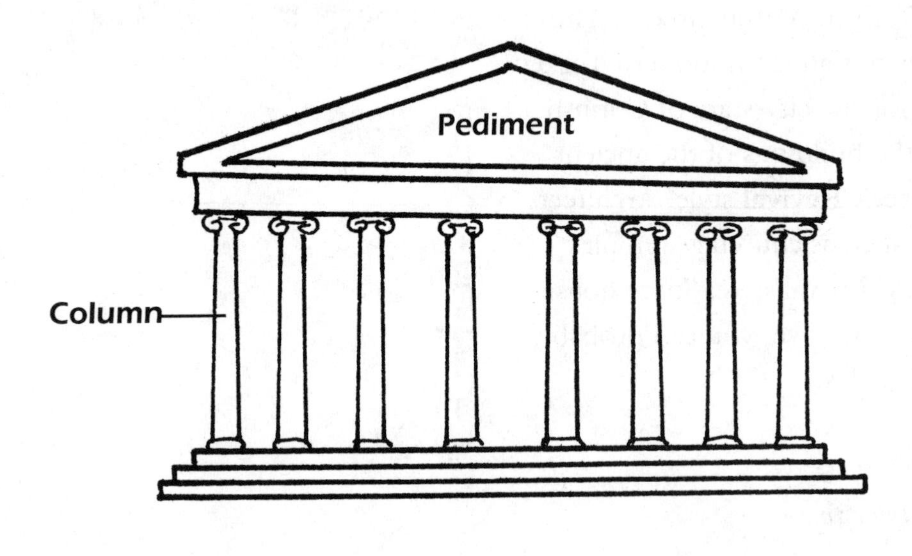

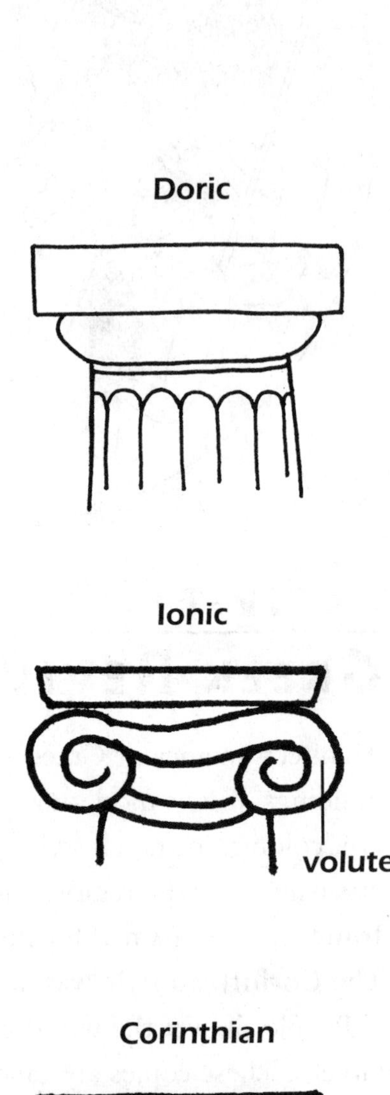

c. *Ornament.* The Greeks liked to decorate their buildings with carved and painted designs. Some of their most popular designs are shown here.

acanthus leaf

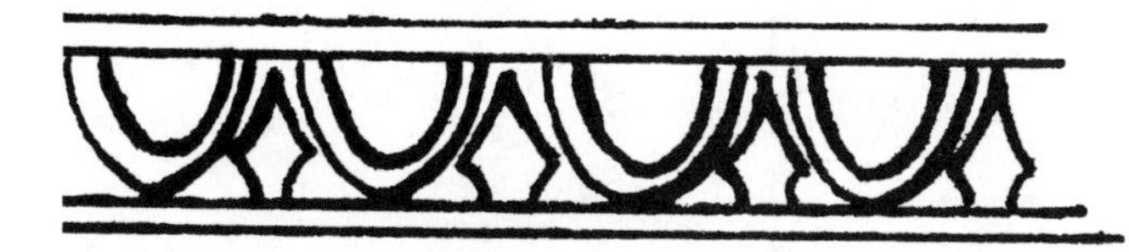

egg and dart

bead and wheel

dentil (toothlike)

Greek key

3. Each player gets one point for each building found. Keep track of the points with a pencil and a pad of paper. The player with the most points wins.

The Parthenon

The leader of Athens, named Pericles (PEHR-uh-kleez), had suggested that the people should thank Athena for helping them win their war against the Persians. He suggested they build her a new marble temple with a beautiful statue of Athena herself inside. The citizens agreed and put Pericles in charge of the project to build the new Doric-style temple, which they called the Parthenon. They started building it in 447 B.C. and finished in 432 B.C.

To Helen it seems that everyone in Athens is in the parade. Some people are carrying food for the feast. Others are bringing gifts to offer to the goddess, including cattle and sheep, their horns decorated with wreaths of flowers.

The sun has nearly set as the parade climbs the steep path to the Acropolis, the big hill overlooking Athens. They are getting closer to Athena's huge new temple, called the *Parthenon* (PAR-thuh-nahn). Its red tile roof and white marble columns shine bright in the setting sun.

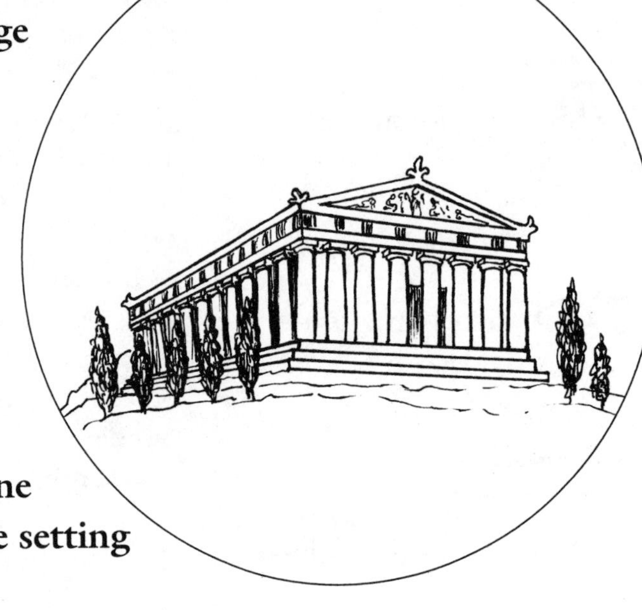

ACTIVITY

Temple Wall Ornament

Greek temples were considered the homes of the gods whose statues were inside. Outside there were altars, where animals were sacrificed.

Your wall ornament will show the front of the temple. You can paint your wall ornament if you want. When the Greek temples were new, their marble and tiles shone bright, and the statues decorating the outside of the temples were painted in brilliant, lifelike colors.

MATERIALS

several sheets of newspaper
pencil
8-by-11-inch (20-by-27.5-cm) piece of thin, noncorrugated cardboard
1 pound (0.5 kg) self-hardening clay
ruler
craft stick or modeling tool
resealable plastic bag
paintbrush (optional)
poster paints in any colors (optional)
water jar filled with water (optional)
12-inch (30-cm) piece of string or ribbon

1. Spread the newspaper over your work area.

2. Copy the outline of the temple front shown on page 88 on the thin cardboard.

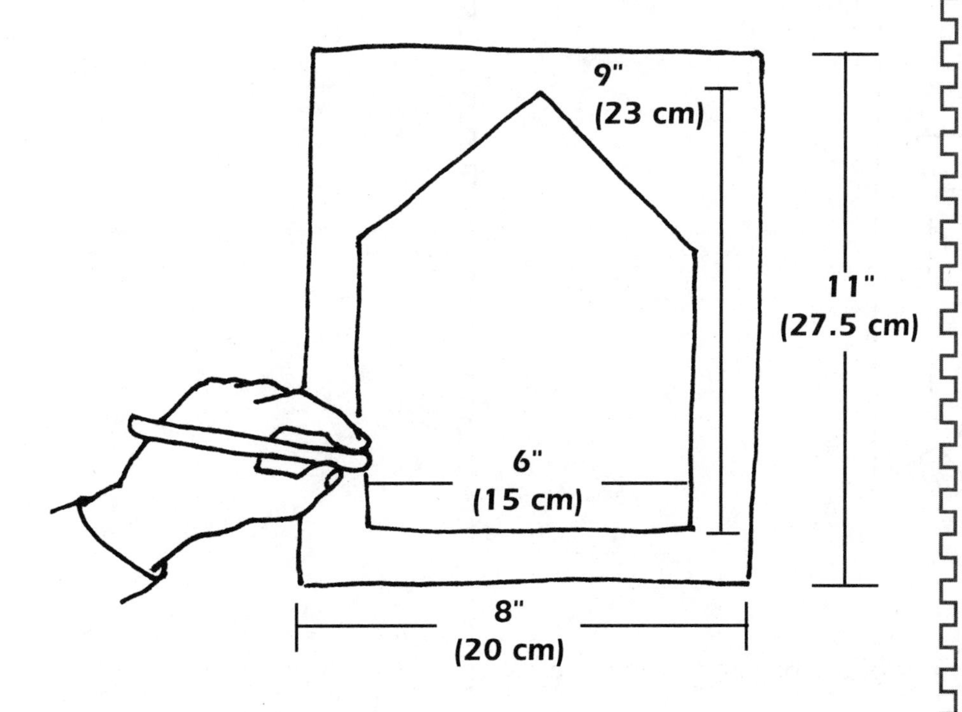

3. Squeeze the clay in your hands until it is soft and feels warm.

4. Roll the clay on the newspaper to form a fat snake shape 11 inches (27.5 cm) long. Use the craft stick to cut off a piece 5 inches (12.5 cm) long. Place this smaller piece of clay in the plastic bag and seal.

5. Place the big piece of clay on your cardboard and press it to make a flat sheet 9 x 6 inches (23 x 15 cm). Press the clay onto the cardboard.

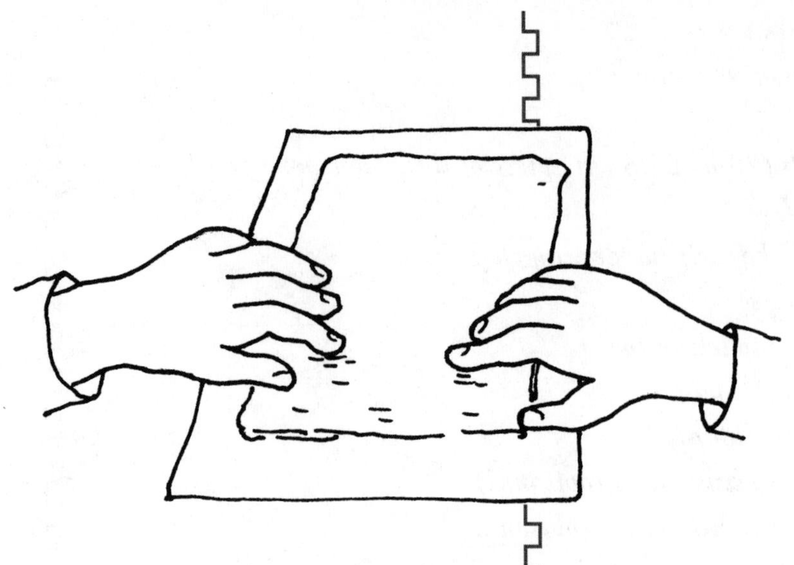

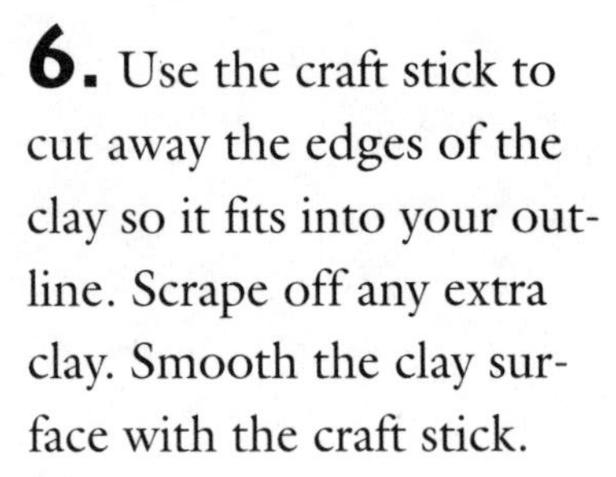

6. Use the craft stick to cut away the edges of the clay so it fits into your outline. Scrape off any extra clay. Smooth the clay surface with the craft stick.

7. Use the craft stick to draw two lines across the temple where the roof begins. Draw the outlines of four columns, as shown.

8. Take the small piece of clay out of the bag and divide it into six equal pieces.

9. Make the columns.

a. Take four of the clay pieces. Press each one to fit the outline of a column.

b. With the craft stick, draw flutes down each column.

c. At the top of each column, use the craft stick to cut and shape the clay into a Doric capital, as shown.

10. Take the fifth small piece of clay and roll it out until it is big enough to fit on the temple as the pediment, the triangular area under the roof. Press it onto the temple and scrape away any extra clay.

11. Take the last small piece of clay and decorate the pediment with raised designs, as shown.

12. Make a hole in the top center of the roof with the pencil.

13. Keep your wall ornament on the cardboard and newspaper. Allow the clay to dry for 2 days, away from sunshine, radiators, or other sources of heat.

14. (Optional) Paint your wall ornament when it is dry. Paint the roof red and the rest of the temple white. Decorate it with other colors if you like.

15. Thread the string through the hole in the top center. Tie a knot in the string and hang your ornament on the wall.

CHAPTER • 11

ATHENA'S FEAST

The parade finally reaches the top of the Acropolis. Penelope and Helen walk up the steps of the temple where the life-size statue of Athena is kept. Helen and three other girls carry the peplos to the temple door, where Athena's priests and priestesses are waiting.

Two priestesses take the peplos from Helen and the girls. They unfold it and hold it up so everyone can see. The golden wool seems to glow in the sunset, and the pictures woven down the front make a handsome pattern. Helen holds her breath as the chief priestess comes over to look closely at the robe.

The priestess tells Helen she has done well. Helen's eyes fill with happy tears. All her worries about the peplos were for nothing! The priests and priestesses go inside the temple to put the peplos on the statue. Helen and Penelope get back in line, and the parade moves on.

The parade ends with a sacrifice at the altar outside the Parthenon. When the ceremony is over, Penelope finds a good place for dinner and spreads out a blanket. Myron and Alexander join Cassandra in unpacking the food they have brought.

Penelope arranges the food on the blanket and invites them all to gather around and begin. Before they eat, Philip reminds them to honor the goddess Athena with a *libation*, an offering of wine to the gods.

They all stand and pour a little wine from their cups onto the ground as they sing a hymn of praise to Athena. Then Penelope passes around a plate of appetizers—hard-boiled eggs, olives, hummus, and bread.

Food and Drink

As a Greek boy or girl, you most often ate bread, vegetables, and fish, along with goat cheese, olives and olive oil, fruits, nuts, and honey. Meat was a rare treat that you ate only on holidays. You ate with a knife and spoon—you did not have a fork. You mostly drank water and goat's milk, but sometimes you drank wine with water added to it. Even as an adult you thinned wine with water.

Men dined only with other men, and women dined only with other women. The only time both men and women dined together was at family meals and festivals.

At parties, slaves served while musicians, dancers, and tumblers entertained. After dinner, men sometimes gathered for a party called a **symposium,** where they drank wine and discussed philosophy until late in the night.

ACTIVITY

MEZE

The Greeks still enjoy starting dinner by nibbling a plateful of fresh, tasty, cold foods, which they call **meze** (meh-ZAY). Some special ingredients are pita (PEE-tuh) bread, which is a flat, unrisen bread; feta (FEH-tuh) cheese, which is a soft cheese made from goat's milk; and hummus (HUM-muss), which is a spread made from chickpeas.

This appetizer recipe serves four people. The plate is divided into four sections, and the food is divided equally among the sections.

INGREDIENTS

¼ pound (100 g) hummus or cottage cheese
1 pita bread
4 green onions
¼ pound (100 g) feta or Swiss cheese
2 hard-boiled eggs
fresh parsley
8 olives
8 mushrooms
4 radishes
small can of tuna fish (optional)

TOOLS

spoon
small bowl
large plate
table knife
4 small table knives
4 small plates

1. Spoon the hummus into the bowl. Place the bowl in the center of the large plate.

2. Break the pita bread into small pieces. Place the pieces on the plate closely around the bowl of hummus.

3. Lay one green onion across the plate with the white end touching the pita bread and the green end facing the edge of the plate. Lay the other three onions on the plate to divide the plate into four equal sections.

4. Use the table knife to cut the feta cheese into four pieces. Place one piece in each section of the plate.

5. Cut the eggs in half with the table knife. Place a half in each section of the plate.

6. Tear the parsley into small pieces and sprinkle it on top of the eggs.

7. Divide the olives, mushrooms, and radishes evenly between the four sections of the plate.

8. (Optional) Spoon an even amount of tuna fish onto each part of the plate.

9. To serve:
a. Give each person a small plate and knife.
b. Eat the appetizers by using a small knife to put hummus, cheese, or tuna fish on pieces of pita bread.
c. Pick up the other foods with your fingers.
d. Enjoy your Greek appetizer plate!

It is beginning to grow dark, and across the hillside oil lamps make bright little islands of light, small copies of the stars overhead. Helen tries to count the stars and gives up. She tells Alexander that there must be more stars in the sky than there are islands in Greece. Alexander laughs and tells her that of course there are.

They finish the feast with dessert, a honey cake and fruit, washed down with more wine and water. Alexander eats so much that Myron tells him he won't be able to walk home! After enjoying their delicious dinner, the tired family collect their things. They wearily head home after a long and joyous day.

ACTIVITY

CHICKEN DINNER

The ancient Greeks usually ate meat only on feast days, when they sacrificed an animal to the gods. They burned part of the meat (this was the gods' part) and ate the rest.

This dinner serves four people.

INGREDIENTS

16 grilled chicken wings or legs (Buy cooked chicken from a store or restaurant.)
1 pound (0.5 kg) coleslaw
loaf of sourdough or other chewy bread
½ cup (125 ml) olive oil

TOOLS

microwave-safe plate
microwave oven
oven mitts
4 plates
spoon
small bowl

1. If the chicken is cold, ask an adult to heat it on a plate in a microwave oven for 3 minutes or until warm. (Be sure to wear oven mitts when removing the plate from the microwave.)

2. Put four pieces of chicken on each plate.

3. Spoon one-fourth of the coleslaw onto each plate.

4. Pour the olive oil into a small bowl.

5. To serve:
a. Give each person a plate.
b. Put the loaf of bread and the bowl of olive oil in the center of the table.
c. Each person should break off a piece of bread and dip it in the olive oil to eat with the chicken and coleslaw.
d. Enjoy your Greek chicken dinner!

ACTIVITY

Greek Dessert

We might find it hard to go for even one day without eating some sugar—but the ancient Greeks had no sugar at all! Honey was their only sweetener. For dessert, they enjoyed honey cakes, fruit, and nuts.

This dinner serves four people.

INGREDIENTS

4 slices of pound cake or other plain cake
½ cup (125 ml) honey
1 tablespoon (15 ml) sesame seeds
8 walnuts or almonds (optional)
4 or more pieces of the following fruit: small bunches of grapes, apples, pears, and figs

TOOLS

4 small plates
small glass bowl
microwave oven
oven mitts
large bowl

1. Place a slice of cake onto each plate.

2. Pour the honey into the glass bowl. Ask an adult to heat it in a microwave oven for 1 minute. (Be sure to wear oven mitts when removing the bowl from the microwave.)

3. Pour the warm honey over each slice of cake, dividing the honey evenly among the four slices.

4. Sprinkle the sesame seeds on the cake, dividing them evenly among the four slices.

5. (Optional) Place two nuts on each slice of cake.

6. Put the fruit in the large bowl.

7. To serve:

a. Give each person a slice of honey cake.

b. Pass the fruit bowl, letting each person choose some fruit.

c. Enjoy your Greek dessert!

Resources

For Children

Roy Burrell and Peter Connolly. *The Greeks.* New York: Oxford University Press, 1990.

Anne Pearson. *Ancient Greece*, Eyewitness Books. New York: Knopf, 1992.

William F. Russell. *Classic Myths to Read Aloud.* New York: Crown Trade Paperbacks, 1989.

For Adults

Jenifer Neils, editor. *Goddess and Polis: The Panathenaic Festival in Ancient Athens.* Princeton, N.J.: Princeton University Press, 1992/Hanover, N.H.: Dartmouth College, Hood Museum of Art, 1992.

For Teachers

A journal, newsletter, reviews of new books, and resources are available from the American Classical League, Miami University, Oxford, Ohio 45056.

For Everyone

Bob Blasidell, *Favorite Greek Myths,* New York: Dover Publications, Inc., 1995.

Perseus. New Haven, Conn.: Yale University Press, 1993. CD-ROM and videodisc. Comprehensive collection of Greek texts and art.

Major museums of art all over the world contain treasures from ancient Greece. Specialized museum resources include Greek and Italic arms and armor at Higgins Armory Museum in Worcester, Massachusetts.

Resources

Glossary

acropolis (uh-KRAH-puh-lus) a fortress on a hill in Greek cities, with strong stone walls enclosing temples; (cap A) the fortress in ancient Athens

agora (AG-guh-ruh) the marketplace in ancient Greek cities

altar in ancient Greece, a table on which animals were sacrificed to the gods

amphora a two-handled clay jar with flared neck, used to hold olive oil

Argonauts a band of Greek sailors who sailed with Jason on the *Argo* to find the Golden Fleece

Athena (uh-THEE-nuh) Greek goddess of wisdom, crafts, and victory in just wars; the goddess of Athens

caduceus (kah-DOO-see-us) a winged staff with snakes, used today to identify medical workers

capital the top part of a column on which the roof rests

chariot a two-wheeled cart pulled by horses

chiton (KYE-tuhn) a linen tunic worn by men and women that was knee-length for men and boys, and ankle-length for women and girls

citizen in ancient Athens, a native-born freeman who could vote in the governing assembly

city-state a self-governing city and the surrounding land that it controlled

clepsydra (KLEP-sye-druh) a water clock

column a pillar that supports the roof of a building

comedy a funny play or story with a happy ending

Corinthian an architectural style characterized by fluted columns and leafy capitals, named after the ancient Greek city-state of Corinth

Crown Games the most prestigious ancient Greek games, at which winners were awarded special wreaths; also called the Panhellenic Games

democracy a political system of rule by the people

discus a round disk made of metal or stone, thrown for distance

Doric an architectural style characterized by fat plain or fluted columns with simple square capitals, named after Doris, a region in ancient Greece

drachma (DRACK-muh) an ancient Greek coin equal to six obols

flute a ridge running down the side of a column

Gorgons in Greek myth, the hideous sisters—Medusa, Euryale, and Stheno—who had snakes for hair

greaves bronze shin guards tied on with leather straps and worn in battle

Greek Revival a style of architecture or design that copies ancient Greek styles

himation (him-MAT-tee-un) an ancient Greek cloak worn by both men and women

hippodrome racetrack

hoplite a heavily armed Greek foot soldier

hydria (HIGH-dree-uh) a three-handled clay pot, used to carry water

Ionic an architectural style characterized by slender fluted columns with capitals carved in volutes, named after the Ionian islands, a region in eastern Greece

javelin a long stick or light spear

kithara (KITH-uh-ruh) a kind of lyre, a stringed musical instrument

klismos (KLIZ-mus) an armless wooden chair with curved back and legs

libation wine poured on the ground as an offering to the gods

lyre a kind of harp

marathon a long-distance race, usually 26 miles and 385 yards (4,537 m) long

meze (meh-ZAY) Greek appetizers

myth a story about gods

obol (AH-buhl) an ancient Greek coin equal to one-sixth of a drachma

Olympic Games the ancient Greek games at Olympia, revived in modern times

owl coin made in ancient Athens that showed Athena on one side and her symbol, the owl, on the other

Panathenaic (pan-uh-thuh-NAY-ick) **Games** the games and parade held at Athens in honor of the goddess Athena's birthday

Panhellenic (pan-huh-LEH-nick) **Games** national games open to all Greeks; also called the Crown Games

Parthenon (PAR-thuh-nahn) the most famous Greek temple, built in Doric style on the Acropolis in honor of Athena in 432 B.C.

pediment a triangular area at the top front and rear of a Greek building

pentathlon (pen-TATH-lun) an athletic contest with five different events (*penta* is Greek for five)

peplos (PEH-plus) a long gown worn by women and girls of ancient Greece

philosophers in ancient Greece, professors who taught all subjects

regatta a boat race

sacrifice something offered to the gods, such as an animal, wine, or a warrior's armor

shrine a site for worship of one or more gods

stater an ancient Greek coin, equal to two drachmas

stoa a long ancient Greek porch used by market sellers and others

symposium an ancient Greek drinking party, at which men discussed philosophy

tragedy a serious play or story that tells about good and evil deeds

trident a three-pronged spear used to catch fish; the symbol of the sea god Poseidon

triremes ancient ships with three rows of oars

volute a spiral hornlike shape that characterizes the Ionic capital

INDEX

D

E

F

G

H

I

J

K

L

M

N

O

P

R

S

T

Z